THE TECH SET

Ellyssa Kroski, Series Editor

P9-APM-329

Library Camps and Unconferences

Steve Lawson

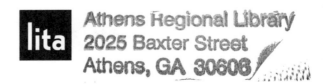

Neal-Schuman Publishers, Inc.

New York   London

Published by Neal-Schuman Publishers, Inc.
100 William St., Suite 2004
New York, NY 10038

Published in cooperation with the Library Information and Technology Association, a division of the American Library Association.

Printed and bound in the United States of America.

The paper used in this publication meets the minimum requirements of American National Standard for Information Sciences—Permanence of Paper for Printed Library Materials, ANSI Z39.48-1992.

ISBN: 978-1-55570-712-5

CONTENTS

Don't miss this book's companion wiki and podcast!

Turn the page for details.

THE TECH SET is more than the book you're holding!

All 10 titles in THE TECH SET series feature three components:

1. the book you're now holding;
2. companion wikis to provide even more details on the topic and keep our coverage of this topic up-to-date; and
3. author podcasts that will extend your knowledge and let you get to know the author even better.

The companion wikis and podcasts can be found at:

techset.wetpaint.com

At **techset.wetpaint.com** you'll be able to go far beyond the printed pages you're now holding and:

- ▶ access regular updates from each author that are packed with new advice and recommended resources;
- ▶ use the wiki's forum to interact, ask questions, and share advice with the authors and your LIS peers; and
- ▶ hear these gurus' own words when you listen to THE TECH SET podcasts.

To receive regular updates about TECH SET technologies and authors, sign up for THE TECH SET Facebook page (**facebook.com/nealschumanpub**) and Twitter (**twitter.com/nealschumanpub**).

For more information on THE TECH SET series and the individual titles, visit **www.neal-schuman.com/techset**.

▶

FOREWORD

Welcome to volume 8 of The Tech Set.

Libraries are embracing a new trend toward participant-driven conferences where sessions are created on-the-fly, topics are discussed spur-of-the-moment, and ideas are free to flourish. *Library Camps and Unconferences* is a one-stop reference manual identifying what it takes to produce one of these informal, yet highly effective participatory events. Author Steve Lawson guides readers through the planning stage, including setting up an event wiki and finding sponsors, and leads them through marketing and implementation, including library camp design and facilitation. Readers will learn about the unconference model from a practical perspective through such topics as creating the day's schedule, encouraging breakout sessions, troubleshooting problems, and configuring rooms.

The idea for The Tech Set book series developed because I perceived a need for a set of practical guidebooks for using today's cutting-edge technologies specifically within libraries. When I give talks and teach courses, what I hear most from librarians who are interested in implementing these new tools in their organizations are questions on how exactly to go about doing it. A lot has been written about the benefits of these new 2.0 social media tools, and at this point librarians are intrigued but they oftentimes don't know where to start.

I envisioned a series of books that would offer accessible, practical information and would encapsulate the spirit of a 23 Things program but go a step further—to teach librarians not only how to use these programs as individual users but also how to plan and implement particular types of library services using them. I thought it was important to discuss the entire life cycle of these initiatives, including everything from what it takes to plan, strategize, and gain buy-in, to how to develop and implement, to how to market and measure the success of these projects. I also wanted them to incorporate a broad range of project ideas and instructions.

Each of the ten books in The Tech Set series was written with this format in mind. Throughout the series, the "Implementation" chapters, chock-full of detailed project instructions, will be of major interest to all readers. These chapters start off with a basic "recipe" for how to effectively use the technology in a library, and then build on that foundation to offer more and more advanced project ideas. I believe that readers of all levels of expertise will find something useful here as the proposed projects and initiatives run the gamut from the basic to the cutting-edge.

I have had the pleasure of hearing Steve Lawson speak at several library events and have been an avid reader of his "See Also…" blog for years. When I found out that he would be co-organizing "Library Camp of the West" in 2008 I knew it would be a resounding success. Steve took that firsthand experience and filled this outstanding book with nuggets of wisdom for achieving every detail of an unconference event. Librarians who are contemplating an informal event of any kind will find Steve's book an all-in-one resource.

Ellyssa Kroski
Information Services Technologist
Barnard College Library
www.ellyssakroski.com
http://oedb.org/blogs/ilibrarian
ellyssakroski@yahoo.com

Ellyssa Kroski is an Information Services Technologist at Barnard College as well as a writer, educator, and international conference speaker. She is an adjunct faculty member at Long Island University, Pratt Institute, and San Jose State University where she teaches LIS students about emerging technologies. Her book *Web 2.0 for Librarians and Information Professionals* was published in February 2008, and she is the creator and Series Editor for The Tech Set 10-volume book series. She blogs at iLibrarian and writes a column called "Stacking the Tech" for *Library Journal*'s Academic Newswire.

PREFACE

Attending a large professional library conference is almost always expensive and time-consuming. Professional conferences can also be, for the lack of a better word, boring. Plenary discussions, paper presentations, keynote speakers—all can seem calculated and mundane. And to tell the truth, not all sessions or meetings prove to be intellectually valuable. The real opportunity for idea exchange takes place during the interactions among people in small groups or one-on-one in hallways, at lunch, or sitting in the hotel lounge.

A "library camp" and an "unconference" are two words for the same idea: they can be thought of as a professional conference that consists entirely of hallway conversations and barroom banter. A library camp is simply an opportunity for library people to get together to talk about libraries—an opportunity that shares many of the characteristics of a large official gathering like the American Library Association Annual Meeting but without the formalities. Library camps blur the distinction between conference "speakers" and "attendees"; they provide a forum where everyone has something to share and everyone has something to learn.

Library camps are typically fee-free for attendees, but they represent freedom in another, more important way by unchaining attendees from committee meetings, from agendas and speaking schedules arranged months in advance, and from huge conference centers and hotels. If you are interested in putting together a library camp, your task is to create an environment that encourages freedom. You will need to provide enough structure so that people know when and where to show up and infrastructure in the form of meeting rooms and perhaps wireless Internet access. You also have to perform something of a balancing act, as the whole point of the "un" in "unconference" is that there isn't too much structure. Your job is to provide the canvas: the entire group will create the painting.

▶ ORGANIZATION AND AUDIENCE

Library Camps and Unconferences is designed to walk all librarians through the process of setting up an unconference, from finding a venue and setting a date, through lining up sponsors and goodies for attendees, to executing the actual day of the event and beyond. In many ways, setting up a library camp is easy. A space of sufficient size and a roomful of librarians ready to exchange ideas are all you need. But going from ideas to reality takes a significant amount of planning and forethought. I draw on examples from my own experience in organizing the Library Camp of the West—an unconference held in Denver in October 2008 for about 100 librarians—and from similar experiences of librarians who have organized or attended library camps across the United States, Canada, and Australia.

Chapter 1 covers the history of library camps and of unconferences in general. It goes over planning considerations, as well as validating any assumptions you may have about unconferences. Chapter 2 covers the most basic requirements for a library camp: a space, a time, and people to plan the event. Technology isn't always at the core of an unconference, but this chapter details how to use Web-based social software, from wikis to instant messaging, to help plan and execute your event. Chapter 3 covers planning the day's schedule as a group. It gives you some ideas on what to expect in the smaller group discussions or breakout sessions and contains advice for how to handle implementation and things that can go wrong. Chapter 4 discusses proper marketing techniques, so the people who are most likely to be interested in the event find out about it. Chapter 5 covers library camp best practices, and Chapter 6 covers ways to measure the success of your library camp.

Library camps and unconferences are supposed to be fun, and while it takes work to organize one, providing a thought-provoking, productive, and friendly atmosphere for librarians in your area can be fun, too. *Library Camps and Unconferences* will help you bring your vision of organizing a library camp to life.

ACKNOWLEDGMENTS

Difficult as it has been, the task of writing this book may be all worth it simply for the chance to thank the following wonderful people in print.

Were it not for my editor Ellyssa Kroski and the people at Neal-Schuman, this book would not exist at all.

I feel very lucky to be part of the Library Society of the World: a group of librarians who get together online and manage to make talking about libraries an engaging and often hilarious activity. The LSW and the larger group of blogging librarians have greatly enriched my professional and personal life, and I am grateful. For their direct contributions to the process of writing this book, I am pleased to thank by name Meredith Farkas, Dorothea Salo, Walt Crawford, Martha Hardy, Joshua M. Neff, Jenna Freedman, David Lee King, John Blyberg, Ryan Deschamps, Stephen Francoeur, Kathryn Greenhill, Michelle Boule, Nicole Engard, and Michael Sauers. I owe special thanks to Iris Jastram for offering perceptive comments on large sections of this book and for generally being a brick.

Laura Crossett and Joe Kraus were ideal co-conspirators on the Library Camp of the West 2008. They helped convert my interest in library camps from hypothetical to actual. John Porcellino was kind enough to donate his artwork to that event and to this book.

I could not ask for more supportive co-workers than the people at Colorado College's Tutt Library.

Last, I owe my greatest thanks to my family: my mom and dad, who have encouraged and supported me through every phase of my life, and Shanon, Luke, and Nicholas, who make everything worthwhile.

▶1

INTRODUCTION: LIBRARY CAMP AND UNCONFERENCE BASICS

- ▶ Origin and Evolution
- ▶ Planning Considerations
- ▶ Assumptions about Unconferences

▶ ORIGIN AND EVOLUTION

To librarians, it may seem that library camps and unconferences appeared out of nowhere with Library Camp 2006 in Ann Arbor, Michigan. While that event is the first widely acknowledged library camp, it stood on the shoulders of two established, related practices: Open Space Technology and BarCamp.

Open Space Technology

The name "Open Space Technology" is something of an oddity. Open Space Technology does not refer to "technology" in the sense of a gadget or a piece of equipment or even something as intangible as software. Instead, Open Space Technology (or, more commonly, Open Space) refers to a practice or method of holding meetings where preexisting agendas and hierarchies are abolished in favor of bringing people together to speak and listen and get to work on the ideas and problems that truly motivate them.

Harrison Owen is the creator and chief standard-bearer for Open Space. Owen has written several books on organizational transformation and leadership, including *Open Space Technology: A*

User's Guide, now in its third edition. In that book, he describes a meeting methodology that he began to create in the 1980s and that he continues to fine-tune. While few library camps have used Open Space methods exactly as described by Owen, most library camps embrace the spirit of Open Space.

In *Open Space Technology: A User's Guide,* Owen (2008) describes a system for bringing together groups of people without an agenda or any other advance preparation to tackle important issues over the span of a day or more. He claims that Open Space works just as well with groups that are small and intimate as with large, diverse groups. Participants are brought together into a large circle where anyone can raise an issue by walking to the center of the circle, stating his or her name and issue, and posting an index card on the wall with the issue written on it. By doing so, the person has created a session on the day's agenda and has taken responsibility for that session.

As we will see later, most library camps have tinkered with this format to some degree when it comes to creating the day's schedule. Many library camps would call themselves "modified" or "hybrid" Open Space events. But even those library camps that diverge from Owen's plan to a large degree still remind participants of the four principles and one law of Open Space. The principles are:

- ▶ Whoever comes is the right people.
- ▶ Whatever happens is the only thing that could have.
- ▶ Whenever it starts is the right time.
- ▶ When it's over, it's over.

"They are," says Owen (2008: 91), "important to the Open Space process, but never to be taken with total seriousness. . . . The principles are simple statements of the way things work in Open Space. In a word, they are descriptive and not prescriptive."

These principles can be very freeing and empowering for librarians experiencing their first unconference and should be comforting to you as you plan your event. Think of the principles when you are worrying about how many people will sign up for the event or if one session will be much more popular than others. Different groups will have different experiences, but trust that whoever takes the initiative to show up is the right group of people.

You may wonder "is it okay if we have three sessions on the same topic?" Or "is it okay if the slot on the schedule says 'Next-Generation Catalogs' but the people in the session spend most of their time talking about staff training?" The second principle says "yes!" Not only is this okay, it is the *only* thing that could possibly happen. The second principle means you don't need to worry that you might be "doing it wrong" because that's impossible.

The last two principles seem to get a little less play at library camps (perhaps it's a professional bias in librarians to value punctuality), but the main point is that if it takes a while to get the day going or to get a session going, that's fine. And if you have an hour allotted but people seem to be talked out after 30 minutes, that's okay too. Take a walk or drop in on another session. If the conversation is still going strong at the end of the hour, interested parties can adjourn to a lobby or café to keep talking. The schedule is not the event: the people and their conversations are the event.

Along with the principles comes the one law of Open Space, the Law of Two Feet:

> If, during our time together, you find yourself in any situation where you are neither learning nor contributing, use your two feet and go to some more productive place. (Owen, 2008: 95)

Many people read the Law of Two Feet and think it is simply a statement of the obvious; it's the practice they normally follow at conferences and events. But for other people, it seems to give them license to do something they wouldn't otherwise do for fear of seeming rude.

Another thing the Law of Two Feet does is make it clear to participants that they are the ones responsible for their own experience. There's no point in blaming speakers or organizers if a session is bad when you can just exercise the Law of Two Feet (and maybe encourage a few other people to follow that law with you) and either check in on another session or hold an impromptu session of your own in a hallway or empty meeting room.

In short, Open Space Technology is a set of guidelines and principles for holding self-organizing, nonhierarchical meetings that are designed to bring together the people who are most motivated and willing to accept responsibility for discussing, planning, and executing solutions for the problems facing a business, organization, or other community. It is appealing to people who want to dispense with the typical structure of a business meeting or professional conference.

BarCamp

Starting in 2003, technology publisher Tim O'Reilly and his company, O'Reilly Media, began holding an annual Open Space–style event called "Foo Camp" (with "Foo" standing for "Friends Of O'Reilly"). Accounts of the first Foo Camp highlight the participants' joy at the opportunity to share ideas with about 200 other technology geeks in a self-organizing, unstructured environment. One session apparently involved taking apart (and rebuilding) a rented hybrid automobile (Rein, 2003).

By 2005, the idea of Foo Camp had caught on, but the event was still invitation-only and limited to about 200 people. In the summer of 2005, a small group of people familiar with Foo Camp decided to put together an alternative event: BarCamp. Planned over the span of a few weeks, the first BarCamp was held in August 2005 in Palo Alto at the same time Foo Camp was happening in Sebastopol, a few hours away up the California coast. Sometimes seen as an anti-Foo Camp, the organizers of the first BarCamp intended it to be a natural, open complement to Foo Camp. As one of BarCamp's creators wrote, "At FOO Camp, someone else invites you and you wonder why; at BarCamp, you invite yourself and over the course of a weekend prove why you did" (Messina, 2006).

While BarCamp wasn't the first or only participant-organized technology conference, the idea and the name caught on. A look at the BarCamp wiki at http://barcamp.org reveals links to hundreds of past events in dozens of countries (all continents except Antarctica are represented) and a sizable list of upcoming BarCamps, PodCamps, BandCamps, DrupalCamps, MomCamps, and so on.

The First Library Camps

The first library camp is widely acknowledged to be Library Camp 2006, which was held at the Ann Arbor District Library (AADL) on April 14 of that year. John Blyberg, who was System Administrator and Lead Developer at AADL at the time, and AADL's Director of Information Technology, Eli Neiburger, were the main organizers of the event at the library, but in a telephone interview (May 4, 2009), Blyberg pointed out that the inspiration for the event came from outside the library. "The idea was brought to our attention by Ed Vielmetti," an Ann Arbor resident with social media and community organizing experience. "We dubbed Ed our 'Superpatron,'" says Blyberg, "and he suggested the Open Space format and suggested that we have a BarCamp-type event."

It's unclear how many people attended that first library camp, and the wiki created for the event now seems to be defunct, but some of the details of the day have been preserved by blog posts from those who were there (Blyberg, 2006b; Atkin, 2006). Discussions seem to have centered mostly around technology and the library: "Bridging the gap" between more and less tech-savvy staff; "Web/Library 2.0"; and "encouraging patron hacking" were among the discussion topics. Atkin (2006) describes a sometimes-confusing environment where sessions ran into one another without clear breaks, and Blyberg (2006b) noted that time flew by so quickly that it was difficult to take notes or to blog the different sessions of the day.

Blyberg was also responsible for the next library unconference, Library Camp East, held at the Darien (Connecticut) Public Library in September 2006. Of the approximately 50 attendees, at least 10 of them wrote blog posts about their experiences, giving the event a good deal of visibility in a larger community of librarians who write and read blogs. The Wikipedia entry for "BarCamp" points out that "the involvement of key figures in the Web development community, such as Tantek Çelik and Ross Mayfield, no doubt helped its adoption" (Wikipedia, 2009). It is safe to say the same about Library Camp. With already-respected and well-known librarians like Blyberg, Jessamyn West, and Casey Bisson writing about Library Camp East, the idea was bound to spread quickly and find an audience of librarians eager to try out something new. If the first library camps seem to have focused heavily on technology, it's likely because the organizers were emulating the BarCamp model, the organizers were technology focused themselves, and the word was spread mostly in blogs, most of the writers and readers of which are technologically adept.

In his blog post about the events of Library Camp East, John Blyberg sets the stage for what would happen in 2007 and 2008 as librarians around the world followed his example. "I still think," he wrote, "that the 'Library Camp' convention can be easily exported to virtually any locale that is convenient enough for a moderately sized group to attend—the critical component, being the people, of course. . . . And who knows, maybe there will be a Library Camp South, West . . . North? We'll see. . . ." (Blyberg, 2006b).

▶ PLANNING CONSIDERATIONS

One of the appeals of the unconference is that it can be many different things; your event can and should be different from other library camps and unconferences. If the event is a work of art, it is up to the unconference participants to paint the picture, but whether they create a detailed miniature or a sweeping mural will depend on the pre-event planning. As you plan your event, you will want to think about what you want to accomplish. Some things may be clear or taken as given from the start of your project, but there are some major areas to keep in mind throughout the planning (see p. 8).

Landmarks in the History of Library Camps
and Unconferences

OCTOBER 2003

Foo Camp: The first "Friends Of O'Reilly" camp was put on by technology publisher Tim O'Reilly and brought the idea of a self-organized conference to the attention of many in the computing and technology field.

AUGUST 2005

BarCamp: Organized quickly as an open counterpart or response to Foo Camp, the BarCamp concept quickly spread, to the point where hundreds of these participatory, technology-focused camps have been held all over the globe.

APRIL 2006

Library Camp 2006, Ann Arbor: Inspired by the BarCamp model, "Superpatron" Edward Vielmetti suggests to Eli Neiburger and John Blyberg at Ann Arbor District Library that AADL hold the first library camp. Subjects are mostly technology-oriented, such as "Bridging the Gap" between library staff who are responsible for technology and those who are not.

SEPTEMBER 2006

Library Camp East, Darien: With Blyberg once again the instigator, the second library camp was held at the Darien Public Library. More well-known library bloggers attended, spreading the idea wider among librarians.

MARCH 2007

L2 Unconference, Melbourne, Australia: Very quickly the library camp or unconference became a worldwide affair, with this Australian conference focusing on Web 2.0 and Library 2.0 concepts.

- ▶ **Participants**: Who will come to your library camp? Do you anticipate that there are certain people or groups who will want to come as soon as they hear about it? Are there other people or groups you really *hope* will come?

- ▶ **Place**: Where will this happen? Do you already have a space in your library that would be appropriate, or do you need to find another location that is more central, larger, cheaper, more open, and so forth?

- ▶ **Theme**: Many library camps don't have a theme besides "let's talk about libraries!" Other library camps have had more or less restrictive themes, such as technology, Library 2.0, the future of libraries, and so on. Would a theme be too limiting, or would it bring focus and attention to your library camp? Could it discourage people who would otherwise attend, or would it motivate people who are specifically interested in your theme?

- ▶ **Size**: How many people can participate? This may be dictated by the size of the space you have available, or, instead, you may need to look for the venue that will accommodate the size of event you really want to hold.

- ▶ **Amenities and perks**: Besides the space, what will you provide for participants? Wireless Internet access? Flip charts and markers? Laptops and projectors for breakout rooms? Snacks? Meals? T-shirts or other souvenirs?

- ▶ **Budget**: Who is going to pay for all this? Library camps are usually done on the cheap, but it is hard to do an event of any size without incurring some costs. Will everything be donated by a host institution? Will you need to find sponsors to cover some expenses? Will attendees need to pay a registration fee? If so, how will you handle the money?

- ▶ **Team**: Who is going to organize this with you? Yes, it's a free-form unconference, but someone has to make sure everything is in place. For smaller events, you may not need more than one person, but having a small group organize the library camp can make it easier (and more fun).

▶ ASSUMPTIONS ABOUT UNCONFERENCES

In this book, I'll repeatedly say that there is more than one way to rock an unconference and that you shouldn't be too hemmed in by worrying about what a library camp "should be" like. At the same time, it will be difficult to talk about library camps or unconferences in general if we don't share a few assumptions about what we are talking about. The following are some of the assumptions I make when writing about library camps and unconferences, assumptions that will mostly go unstated elsewhere in the book:

▶ **Library camps are informal**. For the Library Camp of the West 2008, we said "leave the PowerPoint at home." The emphasis is not on polished presentations but on spontaneity, interaction, and discussion.

▶ **Library camps are participant driven**. This book will focus on what you need to do as an organizer, but, when it comes down to it, library camps are about the participants making the day happen on their own. Like a parent sending a kid off to college, you will need to be ready to let go on the day of the event so that the participants can find their own way.

▶ **Library camps are free or low cost**. Most library camps have been free to attend. Those that do have a registration fee are typically less than traditional conferences ($50.00 or less).

▶ **Library camps are local**. This may be changing as more library camps are folded in as official or unofficial adjuncts to traditional conferences and as larger, established groups and organizations see the potential for unconferences aimed at a national audience. But to date, the typical library camp audience lives within driving distance of the venue.

▶ **Library camps are for all types of libraries and librarians**. Again, this may change as library camps proliferate and diversify, but most unconferences have not focused on one type of library to the exclusion of others. All are welcome.

One other assumption or limitation informs this book, and that is nationality. I live and work in the United States. While some of the examples we'll look at in this book will come from library camps and unconferences in other countries, many of my assumptions will come from thinking of the unconference in an American context.

If the event you have in mind is significantly different from what is outlined above, don't panic! As long as you have good reasons for the choices you make, your event is likely to be a success. Just be aware that the more you differ from this imaginary "typical" unconference, the more you may encounter people who say "that's not an unconference" and the more you may have to explain and make explicit your choices.

The Unconference Is Gently Subversive

Remember that being a bit different and out of the ordinary is one of the great strengths of the library camp. By its nature, the unconference is gently subversive. It is subversive in what it implies about conferences and professional development in general. A library camp says "you don't need a big organization with a lot of dues-paying members to hold a meaningful conference." It says that participants don't need to put in their time on committees or win elections in order to run a meeting. You don't need permission to stand up and share what you know in front of your peers. You don't need to stay inside a box, whether that box is labeled "public library" or "director" or "library school student" or "rural library." All you need to do is show up, listen up, and speak up.

But as subversive as the unconference might be, it is a *gentle* subversion. Few people would argue that library camps are now the only legitimate way to hold a conference or that there is no longer a role for large, established organizations to play in bringing librarians together. The fact that most library camps are open, egalitarian affairs shouldn't imply that there is no place for meetings of just directors or reference librarians or school librarians. The library camp is less a Trotskyist "permanent revolution" and more of an anarchist "Temporary Autonomous Zone." Ideally the unconference provides space for us to let down our guard a bit and to recognize what we all can learn from one another.

Because of this gentle nature, established organizations are less likely to see the unconference as threatening and are more likely to try and co-opt it as a welcome innovation. Inevitably, some organizations will treat it simply as a buzzword and a trendy idea that might catch people's attention. But there is potential for established organizations large and small to internalize a bit of what library camps and unconferences embody—a sense of spontaneity, equality, and togetherness—and that the library camp can bring about a small but recognizable change in the way we work together as coworkers and professionals.

►2

PLANNING

- ► Lay the Groundwork
- ► Get Organized
- ► Map Out the Day's Activities
- ► Provide Equipment, Supplies, and Services
- ► Determine Your Budget and Funding Sources

► LAY THE GROUNDWORK

Playing Host at Your Unconference

"Organizing an unconference" may sound like a contradiction in terms. But if your event is going to be open to more than a handful of people, it will take some concerted effort on your part to make sure that the stage is set for people to interact freely and spontaneously. As an unconference organizer, your job is less like the director of a play and more like a party hostess. The hostess doesn't tell people when to talk or whom to talk to, but she does make sure the house is ready, the drinks are cold, and there are plenty of interesting guests to entertain one another.

Your first concern as a library camp organizer (or camp counselor, if you wish) is to find one or more partners to help you out. It's unlikely you can think of everything on your own, and the larger and more ambitious your event, the happier you will be to spread out the work. After that, you need to find a place big enough to host the kind of event you have in mind and set an appropriate date. Part of setting the date is to be aware of other library conferences and related events so that you don't create scheduling conflicts for your target audience. On the other hand, there is a growing trend to intentionally schedule library camps to coincide with popular existing library conferences and meetings to capitalize on the fact that potentially interested people will already be in that place at that time, ready to talk about libraries. The unconference as preconference, postconference, or shadow conference is a trend to watch.

Finding a Team or Going Solo

If the Open Space Technology principles hold that "whoever comes is the right people" and "whatever happens is the only thing that could have," perhaps we could come up with a corollary that states "whoever organizes an unconference is the only one crazy enough to try it." Most of the time the organizing group will grow organically, but if you go out looking for collaborators, here are some things to keep in mind.

Location

Given the ease of electronic communication, there is no need for you and your collaborators to be in close physical proximity (see Chapter 5 for more on collaborating at a distance). However, having an organizer who is on the staff of the institution that is hosting the event (assuming you are holding the event at a library or related institution) can be a great benefit. At the very least, having someone near the planned location who can see the facilities and deal directly with the people in charge there can save you time and misunderstandings.

Diversity

When gathering collaborators, think about diversity: not necessarily ethnic or gender diversity, but libraryland diversity. If you are aiming to put on a general library camp that appeals to people working in all kinds of libraries, it would be wise to have a group of organizers who do not all come from the same kind of library (e.g., public or academic libraries), not to mention all from the same institution.

It might also be worthwhile to think of geographic diversity if you don't want your event to seem too confined to one community. Once you have someone on the team who is close to the actual library camp site, consider trying to find people who are spread out a bit in your region. For the Library Camp of the West, we had an academic librarian from the host institution, The University of Denver (Joe Kraus); an academic librarian from Colorado Springs (me); and a public/school librarian from a small town in Wyoming (Laura Crossett). This made it clear at a glance that the event was not intended just for people from large Denver-area libraries.

Connections

Think about who your potential collaborators know and who knows them. Especially if you are new to the area or new to the job, it might be worth getting some people on board simply because they are well-connected in the area. I wouldn't suggest that you pursue a well-known librarian just to have her name on the project. Instead, look for that person who has worked on conventional conferences before or is active in the state organization or has done collaborative projects in the past. If you can get that person interested in trying something new with a library camp, you may be able to draw on her organizational experience when it comes to planning the event and on her professional network when it is time to start marketing.

Finding a Space

For some library camps, finding space isn't an issue. If you are working on the Piqua Public Library Library Camp, and it is the director and staff of the library putting together the camp, chances are that the event will be held in the library. Even so, where you hold the event will dictate how the library camp goes. If you have the freedom to choose, you should choose wisely. If your choice has been made up front, you need to be realistic about what your location and event space means to your unconference.

Your first consideration may be large scale: what city or even what state or region should host the library camp? If your options are fairly wide open, the more central the location the better. We chose Denver for the location of the Library Camp of the West because of the concentration of libraries and librarians in Denver and the city suburbs and its relative centrality and ease of access to other cities in Colorado, such as Boulder and Colorado Springs. Even though one of our organizers, Laura Crossett, was from Wyoming, we thought it was much more likely that a small group of Wyoming librarians would join us in Denver than it was that scores of Colorado librarians would make the trek to Wyoming. Now that we have had a successful library camp in Denver, we are looking into having our next event in Wyoming.

If you are working on an unconference where you hope to attract a national audience, think about access to airports and other issues around transportation. People in Nevada might love the idea of a fall conference in New Hampshire, but it would certainly be easier for them to get to Chicago.

A traditional conference is held in a hotel or convention center. Most unconferences won't generate the kind of money that would be needed to lease such a venue. Foregoing the convention center is no hardship, given that the idea of the unconference is to be more personal and less formal than the traditional conference. Some information professionals are uncomfortable with the idea that librarians tend to be so closely identified with large institutions and collections and buildings. And it is true that, for most librarians today, our jobs are more about information and people than they are about buildings. But when you are looking for a place to hold your library camp, you will be happy that you and your collaborators have an inside track to useful real estate.

Of the 25 library camps and unconferences held between 2006 and 2008 and documented on the Library Leadership Network's "Unconference and library camp practices" Web page, 18 of the events were held in a library or on a college (or other school) campus (Crawford, 2009). Of the remaining seven, one was organized and sponsored by a university, though held off-campus, and another was a very small event held in a hotel meeting suite. Clearly, for most library camps, space in the library or the parent institution is the easiest space to get.

This doesn't mean that any library space will do. Your needs will vary depending on what you have planned, but for a typical library camp you will need at least one large room that can fit everyone attending the conference (see Figure 2.1), as well as a group of breakout rooms of varying sizes.

A breakout session is where the larger group "breaks out" into smaller groups, usually based on shared interests. For an unconference, a "breakout session" is pretty much the same thing as a "session" you might have at a regular conference.

If you try to hold the event without the large meeting room, no one will be able to address the entire group at once, and some of the usual library camp practices—such as having the group work

▶ Figure 2.1: Library Camp of the West Opening Session

together to set the day's schedule and having a group wrap-up session at the end of the day—will be impossible. Likewise, if you don't have breakout rooms at your disposal, you will need to either have a single-track conference where everyone is participating in the same discussion for the entire day or have groups break out for discussion at separate tables or areas of the large room, which can lead to noise problems. None of this means that you *need* to have a big room and several small rooms, but it does mean that the kind of space you reserve will have a large impact on the kind of library camp you will be able to hold.

Just because libraries and colleges have the kind of space you need and are likely to be interested in hosting a library camp, it doesn't necessarily follow that the space will be free. If you are putting on your event with the cooperation of an academic department (such as a library and information science graduate department), it might have some classroom space that it schedules and controls. If, instead, you are using the school's more general purpose meeting rooms such as you might find in the college or university student center, expect that the school will "charge back" the sponsoring department. Make sure you understand up front exactly what the space will cost and how much your sponsor is willing to cover.

Setting a Date

There is no easy formula for setting a date. Every date is bound to be bad for someone, but there are a few rules of thumb.

Do not put your library camp up against a major national or regional conference (unless, of course, your event will be *part* of a larger traditional conference. See the next section on unconferences as preconferences). In the United States, the main event each year is the American Library Association's Annual Conference in June or July. You can find the date for the ALA Annual along with other major ALA-affiliated events (such as the Public Library Association National Conference, Association of College and Research Libraries National Conference, and the Library and Information

Technology Association National Forum) on the American Libraries Calendar section of the ALA Web site.

Of course, you will want to check your regional calendars, too. In the United States, check with your state library association to see when their annual meeting will be.

Looking back at the Library Leadership Network's "Unconference and library camp practices" for 2006–2008, there seems to be no one day of the week that people have settled on for library camps (Crawford, 2009). Most of them were held on weekdays, suggesting that organizers were confident that attendees could get leave from work to attend.

Most of the past library camps or events scheduled for 2009 listed on the LISWiki "Library Camp" page have been single-day events, and none of them is longer than two days (LISWiki, accessed 2010). Many of the multiple-day events have a broader focus than just libraries, such as THATCamp (The Humanities and Technology Camp) 2009 or InfoCamp Seattle 2009. It is worth considering making your camp a multiple-day event. At the end of Library Camp of the West, many of the participants said they wished they could come back the next day to continue sharing ideas and getting to work on actually implementing some of the ideas that had come up during the unconference. An additional day can lead to a more diverse schedule. You may feel less wary of adding keynotes, scheduled talks or panels, or other sessions arranged in advance if you know that it isn't eating into your one day of unconference time.

An additional day of conferencing also means an additional day of reserving (and possibly paying for) space, an additional day's worth of meals and breaks, and an additional task of facilitating overnight stays for some of your participants. The multiple-day event might be most attractive when—as with the two-day Seattle Zine Unconference and two-day LITACamp, both in 2009—you anticipate that a large number of your participants are coming from out of state. When people are already flying in and booking hotels, a multiple-day event is likely to be more attractive to them than a single day would be, as an extra night in a hotel is just a small part of their conference budget.

Scheduling the Unconference as a Preconference

A trend to watch is the idea of the unconference-as-preconference (or postconference or parallel conference or alternative conference). The logic is relatively simple: if there is a sizable group of librarians who are already traveling to be at an established "official" library conference, might they be willing to extend their trip by one day to attend an unconference as well? I spoke to Jenna Freedman (phone communication, March 24, 2009), a reference librarian and curator of the zine collection at Barnard College, about the two unconferences she helped plan to coincide with the Association of College and Research Libraries (ACRL) Conference in March 2009 in Seattle. The first, the Radical Reference ACRL Unconference (see Figure 2.2), was a small event geared for members of the Radical Reference group, or anyone else wanting to discuss "social justice and alternative and radical collections and programs in academic libraries" (ACRL Unconference 2009, accessed 2009). The second, the Zine Librarian (Un)conference,

▶ Figure 2.2: Radref Scheduling (Photo of Lia Friedman by Jenna Freedman; www.flickr.com/photos/jennafreedman/3364149008/)

was a larger two-day event that mixed prescheduled sessions and unconference sessions.

By timing the events to coincide with an established national conference, Freedman said they were able to pull in librarians who otherwise wouldn't have been able to attend. Scheduling the Radical Reference unconference as an unofficial ACRL preconference "was totally effective in getting academic librarians to attend," said Freedman. "We had a small turnout that was bolstered by ACRL. People from Wellesley, say, would never have been able to attend an unconference in Seattle otherwise." What is true of ACRL is true of any national conference. Why not a Medical Library Camp coinciding with the Medical Library Association Annual Meeting or a SpecialCamp before the Special Libraries Association Annual Conference?

At the same time, a preconference can attract local librarians who cannot afford or do not want to attend the major event or who want to extend their professional development from the official conference through less-formal discussions with a more local focus. At both of the Seattle unconferences, Freedman said local librarians and library school students mixed easily with the people from out of town.

If your library camp is going to be run as an official add-on to an established conference—"official" as in sponsored by the organization that is hosting the larger conference—some of your decisions about venue, food, and other elements of the library camp may be decided for you and arranged and even paid for by the host organization. This can be a huge advantage if the organization will be absorbing the costs, but be sure to get in writing exactly who is arranging and paying for what. If a national library association is paying for the space in the conference hotel, that seems like a great deal, but if you are stuck paying for hotel catering, audiovisual services, and wireless Internet, you may find that this isn't much of a deal after all.

▶ GET ORGANIZED

Library camps often are not high-tech affairs. The emphasis on the day of the event is on making face-to-face human connections. It's easy to envision a successful library camp that uses no technology more complicated than a whiteboard or flip chart with markers.

Even if a library camp does not depend on technology on the day of the event, it is not a coincidence that library camps have become popular in the age of social software. As Clay Shirky writes in his book, *Here Comes Everybody: The Power of Organizing Without Organizations*, social software has made it trivially easy for groups to form and act online:

> By making it easier for groups to self-assemble and for individuals to contribute to group effort without requiring formal management (and its attendant overhead), these tools have radically altered the old limits on the size, sophistication, and scope of unsupervised effort. . . . And as we would expect, when desire is high and costs have collapsed, the number of such groups is skyrocketing, and the kinds of effects they are having on the world are spreading. (Shirky, 2008: 21)

Social software might still be valuable on the day of the library camp, but you will find it more useful as a tool to plan, promote, and archive your event. In this section, we will examine some of the many tools available to the library camp planner and look at how they have been used by various unconferences in the past.

Recommending or even just writing intelligently about specific social software sites is made difficult by the fact that these sites are changing all the time. Features come and go; sites themselves come and go. A site that has few features and fewer users at the time of this writing could quickly gain both, while a site that seems perfectly suited for library camp planners today could make ill-advised changes to their interface or service model tomorrow. Even a giant like Google, which shows no signs at the time I am writing this that they are in any danger of going out of business, has been pulling the plug on projects like Google Video, Jaiku, and Dodge-ball.

You will need the means for camp organizers to chat and post information in advance of the event. You will need ways for participants to communicate with one another and post notes and results of their discussions. Right now, the solution might involve a wiki, or Google Docs, or Meebo chat rooms, but a year from now, you might find a completely different set of Web sites and services that do the same thing or accomplish the same ends.

The Wiki as a Conference Site

A wiki is a Web site that is easy to edit and to open up for collaboration by groups large and small. The name "wiki" comes from the Hawaiian word for "quick" and is a sign of the wiki's chief virtue: updates and changes can be made quickly and easily.

By now, most librarians are familiar with wikis because of the prominence of Wikipedia. But not all wikis need to be huge, sprawling, and encyclopedic, nor do they all need to be editable by anyone in the world with Internet access and with an axe to grind. We'll look at how a wiki can be useful as your unconference site, but for more information about using a wiki, choosing a free wiki site, hosting your own, and seeing how other people have used wikis as official or unofficial supplements for traditional conference sites, see Lauren Pressley's *Wikis for Libraries,* which is another volume in The Tech Set series.

The wiki has become the standard for library camp Web sites because of the ease of adding and editing information (see Figure 2.3). In fact, the wiki is an online expression of the ethos of the unconference. Where the unconference allows all participants a voice, the wiki allows all participants to edit pages. Where the unconference seeks to blur the boundary between presenter and audience, the wiki blurs the boundary between writer and reader.

There are other ways of putting content online quickly, such as a blog, or—for those who are more technically adept—a content-management tool like Drupal or Joomla. But the wiki has several important advantages over these solutions:

▶ Figure 2.3: Library Camp Kansas Homepage

▶ **Ease of setup**: Most hosted wikis ("hosted" meaning you sign up for an account on a wiki site rather than install software on your own server) can be ready to go after a very quick sign-up form. Many sites provide hosted wikis. Some of the most popular among previous library camps have been PBWorks.com (formerly PBWiki), Wetpaint.com, and Wikispaces.com. Groups that host their own wiki tend to favor MediaWiki (the software originally developed to support Wikipedia). By hosting their own wiki, they sacrifice the ease of setting up an account for the total control over the site (assuming they know what they are doing).

▶ **Ease of editing**: To edit a wiki page, typically users just click an "Edit" link or button on the page they want to change. Adding new pages is similarly easy. Most wikis have What You See Is What You Get (WYSIWYG) editing modes, while others have easy-to-learn conventions for making headings, links, images, and so on. Wikis typically have help pages and "sandbox" pages where users can try out editing a mock wiki page before making edits to real pages.

▶ **Ease of collaboration**: Unlike a blog, where there are a series of individual posts, usually by a single author, the wiki makes it easy for one author to start a page and many other authors to add information later. This is important for your unconference site, as you will want all participants to chip in to improve pages and add information.

Seeding the Wiki

Experience shows that while people are often happy to contribute to a wiki, they may feel intimidated if they are presented with a blank slate. As the library camp organizer, it is up to you to create some of the most important pages on the wiki and prime the pump in some cases by adding a little information to get things started. Here are some pages you would want to create from the outset:

▶ **Homepage**: The homepage of the library camp wiki should contain the name of the event; the date, start and end times, and location; a brief statement of what your library camp is all about; an explanation of what an unconference is (or a link to an explanation); instructions on how to get an account on the wiki and edit the site; and links to the other major wiki pages you have created. Assume that people aren't sure what a "library camp" is supposed to be, and give them a little taste of what to expect right up front.

▶ **Registration page**: Many unconferences have people "register" just by putting their name on a list on the wiki. You should sign yourself up, so people have a model to follow (such as putting their name, institution, and e-mail contact information). If your event requires something more closed or formal (e.g., if you are charging admission or have a very limited number of spots available and want people to contact an organizer first), you will still need a page on the wiki that explains the registration process and directs participants to the proper place. Even if you do have a more formal registration process, you should consider having a page where you list attendees by name. When people see that others have signed up, it will encourage them to put their names down, too.

▶ **Tentative schedule**: Show people how the day will break down. Of course you won't have sessions planned yet, but this is the place to show what you will come up with shortly (see the later section, "Map Out the Day's Activities"): when participants should expect to see the full-group sessions, breakout sessions, keynotes or other planned presentations if you have any, breaks, and so on.

▶ **Directions and parking**: Consider using one of the many on-line mapping sites (like Google Maps or Yahoo! Maps) to create a link to a map of the area, or embed the map in your wiki page. Parking can be a source of anxiety for many people, so spell out what they should expect.

▶ **Suggested discussion topics**: Even if you are planning to create the actual schedule on the day of the event, a "discussion topics" page can get people's ideas flowing ahead of time and can serve as a spark and an advertisement for the library camp as people think about the possibilities (see Figure 2.4). At Library Camp of the West 2008, one of the most popular sessions was "Impractical, Unfeasible, Unfundable Ideas," a session that was suggested on the wiki by a person who ended up being unable to come on the day of the event. Participants still loved the idea, and we ran with it anyway.

▶ **Online coverage of your library camp**: This page can possibly wait until later, but you will want to keep track of what people are saying on the Web about the event. A page that has links to blog posts, photos, and other off-wiki content or coverage of the unconference is a nice touch.

Creating Editors

There is not much point in creating a wiki if the camp organizers are the only people who can edit the site. How you enable people to become editors will vary based on the software you choose, but I encourage you to be as open about it as you can. For the Library Camp of the West, we put the wiki password right on every page of

▶ Figure 2.4: Suggested Discussion Topics Page for Library Camp Nebraska

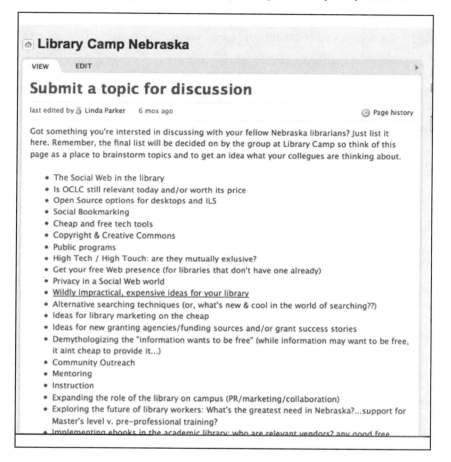

the site. We took the added precaution of using a slightly distorted JPEG image of the password rather than putting the text on the page so that the password could not potentially be read by spam-bots. Even having the password in clear view on every page of the wiki, we didn't have a single case of spam or vandalism.

Wiki sites seem to be moving away from having a single password for all users, as we did for Library Camp of the West, and toward systems that require users to register an account before they edit. In that case, it again makes sense to be as open as you can at first. If there is a setting to allow anyone to register, try that first. You should always be able to delete accounts from troublesome users or switch to a more restrictive method for registering new users where you will have to approve them before they can edit.

If, for whatever reason, you need to approve users before they can edit the site, be sure to review new account requests as promptly as possible. You don't want the library camp to lose steam while a queue of participant requests builds up in your e-mail.

Backing Up the Wiki

Any wiki site you sign up for or software you install on your own server should allow you to back up the data. Use that feature early and often. For small problems or nuisances, you can use the "revert" feature of the wiki to go back to a previously saved version, but for larger problems or outright failures, you will want a complete backup of all the pages (and all the revisions, if you can). One caution: there is no standard data format or markup convention among wiki software, so it would not be an easy task to take your backup from one wiki software and upload it to another.

Growing Your Library Camp Wiki

Ideally, your wiki will evolve as time goes on. When you first start the site, the organizers will be the only people putting up much content. In fact, it is possible to use the wiki as your main base of operations, putting up information about the budget, scheduled chats, calls or meetings, deadlines for the organizers, and so on. Even if you decide to keep that communication off the public site, it will still be true that, at first, it will be just you and your collaborators starting new pages and outlining what you expect to happen.

As more people sign up, more will be motivated to update the wiki. That's one good thing about having the registration be a simple wiki page. To get registered, people have to figure out the wiki, and once they have done that, they might as well hit another page and add some information there. With the right encouragement and motivation, you will have participants soon updating the Suggested Topics page, signing up to volunteer on the day of the event (see Figure 2.5), and perhaps even creating new pages for things like ride and room sharing.

▶ Figure 2.5: Practical Jobs Wiki Page for the 2008 Western Australia Web 2 Unconference

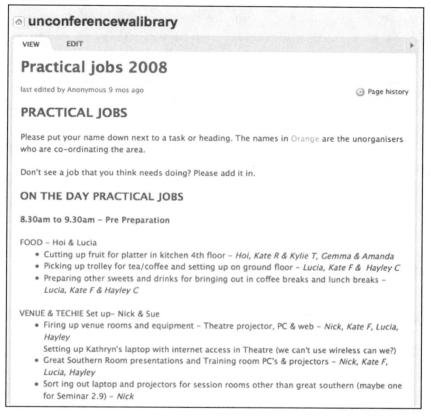

Any good wiki site or software will have notification features (generally RSS feeds or e-mail) to alert you when changes have been made on the wiki. It can seem like a bit much to get an e-mail every time someone changes a comma, but it is exciting to get reminders that people are not only finding and reading the site but also adding to it and editing it. Notifications will also help you keep an eye on the site so you can stamp out any spam or abuse and remind you to go back and update pages in response to useful material added by others.

On the day of the event, assuming that you have wireless Internet available to the camp, you should encourage people to post notes as they take them on the various sessions. If your group is particularly technology oriented, with most people having laptops or other wireless devices, you can even use the wiki as the main mass communications medium for the day, adjusting the schedule in real time, putting announcements on the front page, and so on. This may require some real-time negotiation, as usually only one person at a time can edit a given wiki page. Most library groups won't have enough people with laptops to make this feasible, but you should still encourage those who can to upload notes and minutes of the sessions to the wiki as soon as possible.

If you are lucky, and your unconference participants continue to want to share information after the end of the event, you'll find that the wiki continues to grow even after the camp is over. People post notes, add their thoughts to existing pages, add links to blog posts or photos about the event, and so on. And even after that activity has calmed down, a relatively static wiki still stands as evidence of the community that your camp brought into being that day and will serve as inspiration for future library camps.

Document Sharing with Google Docs

The unconference wiki is a great collaborative space, but it might be unwise for the library camp organizers to have all their collaboration out in the open for anyone to see. And while you may not need formal minutes of your meetings and discussions (whether they take place in person, via e-mail, or through chat), it is likely that you will want a place to keep track of the things you have decided on, things you have yet to do, and shared language for things like pitches to vendors for sponsorship. It is also likely that you will need a place to keep track of donations, whether they take the form of cash or donations of goods, services, space, and the like.

Most librarians are comfortable with standard productivity software like Microsoft Office's Word and Excel. It is tempting to use these familiar tools to create your spreadsheet and to-do lists and so on. But these kinds of documents can be difficult to use collaboratively. If you have more than one or two people on your planning team, it can be hard to be sure that you are looking at the most recent version of the document. If two people edit the document at the same time, they will be working on separate copies, making the job of reconciling their changes more difficult. To get around all this, several companies have made it possible to collaborate on documents hosted on the Web, using their own editing software. One of the most popular is Google Docs (available at http://docs.google.com), a free component of a person's free Google account.

For the Library Camp of the West, we found that a few shared documents on Google Docs were enough to keep us all on the same page (see Figure 2.6). We had a single text document where we would share questions, worries, to-do lists, and the like. We had a spreadsheet where we did the most basic kind of accounting of expenses and donations. And we had a few miscellaneous documents of lists of possible vendors for our giveaway, lists of logins for the wireless network, and a sample invoice that we could use to send to vendors who had expressed interest in donating money.

▶ Figure 2.6: Google Docs Planning Page for Library Camp of the West 2008

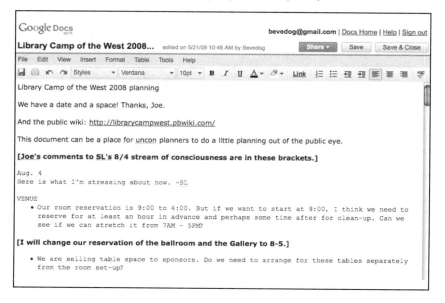

▶ MAP OUT THE DAY'S ACTIVITIES

Just because the participants will come up with their own session topics does not mean that you are done planning once you reserve some space and set up a wiki. You still have many decisions to make and plans to put in place. Will your event have a theme? Will all the sessions be scheduled on the day of the event (see Chapter 3 for more on creating the schedule of sessions), or will you have an invited keynote speaker or other sessions planned in advance? Are you providing lunch or snacks? There really is a lot more to a library camp than the discussion sessions, so be ready to plan ahead to shape the day for your unconference.

The Basic Outline Schedule

Even the most open event, where all the session topics will be decided upon at the library camp itself, still needs an outline schedule. The outline schedule will help potential participants understand how the day is supposed to go and will keep you on track on the day of the unconference. The most basic schedule for a one-day event will start with an all-group session to create the agenda; have three or four time slots for multiple parallel breakout sessions that take up the bulk of the day; and finish with another all-group session to wrap up. Somewhere in that schedule would be a lunch break and probably one or more shorter morning and afternoon breaks as well.

So, a very simple schedule—based on the schedule we used for the Library Camp of the West 2008—looks like this:

8:00–9:00	Registration, arrival
9:00–10:00	Group session, create schedule
10:15–11:30	Breakout I
11:30–1:00	Lunch
1:00–2:00	Breakout II
2:00–2:30	Coffee break
2:30–3:30	Breakout III
3:30–4:30	Group session, wrap up

This may look like a "light" schedule with only about three hours of meeting times. It would be possible to condense some of the breaks and group sessions and get another breakout session in. But remember, one of the ideas of the unconference is that the less-structured time—the breaks, the meals, and so on—is not wasted time. Participants will continue to talk and think and network and form valuable professional and social relationships during those times, even more so than during the sessions.

If you decide to add more structured, prescheduled sessions, you can start the day with a keynote and follow that with lightning talks or pecha kucha sessions (both of these are covered later in this chapter) and reserve the afternoon for your Open Space–style sessions. If you are featuring more conventional presentations and panels as well as open discussions, it's possible to mix them in the schedule among the breakout sessions, like a "track" at a conventional conference (see Figure 2.7).

▶ Figure 2.7: Library Camp of the West 2008 Basic Schedule

librarycampwest

VIEW   EDIT   ▸

Schedule

last edited by Steve Lawson   7 mos ago   Page history

The schedule for the Unconference on October the 10th will be outlined before the Library Camp and will likely include all-camp meetings at the beginning and end of the day with morning and afternoon breakout sessions and a lunch break. But we haven't gotten that far yet.

So far our intrepid camp counselors have come up with a possible rough schedule for the day, which you can see below. If you have any opinions on the subject (more breakout sessions? more coffee?), please leave comments below or write to one of the Camp organizers.

8:00 – 10:00	Light breakfast and coffee during check-in and program discussion
8:00 – 9:00	Check-in, mill around, introduce yourself
9:00 – 10:00	Introductions and creating detailed program (see Suggested topics) with room assignments (see Meeting rooms)
10:15 – 11:30	Breakout session #1
11:30 – 1:00	Lunch (Not provided. See the wiki page for lunch suggestions.)
1:00 – 2:00	Breakout session #2
2:00	Afternoon snack (cookies, soft drinks) served
2:15 – 3:15	Breakout session #3
3:15 – 4:00	Regroup, wrapup

Camp and Unconference Themes

Of course any library camp already has a theme: libraries! But some library camps are also built around a more specific theme. Technology-related themes are popular but are not the only kinds of themed library camps that have been successful.

- The L2 Unconference in Melbourne and Library 2.0 on the Loose in Perth were two Australian unconferences that took Library 2.0 as a theme. Topics discussed included online social networks, Web 2.0 applications in libraries, changes to library catalogs, gaming in libraries, and staff training to meet the demands of Library 2.0.
- RepoCamp was an unconference for people who are "interested in managing and creating digital repository software and their contents." Sessions were mostly about software that supports digital repositories and included prototyping sessions where participants worked on software prototypes to enter in a competition.
- Mashed Libraries UK 2008 was devoted to library applications of mashups: the programming practice of bringing data together from multiple online sources to create a new service.
- The Radical Reference group hosted an unconference as an unofficial preconference to the 2009 Association of College and Research Libraries meeting in Seattle. The meeting focused on "social justice and alternative and radical collections and programs in academic libraries" and included a session where participants worked together to answer real reference questions that had been submitted to the Radical Reference Web site.

Many good things can come out of having a theme for your library camp. You can expect that participants will have a more focused experience. Rather than having sessions that range widely from high-tech topics to community and personnel issues, a themed camp will keep participants talking about issues around a single agreed upon topic. There will be more carryover from one session to another, and participants may feel comfortable with less uncertainty about what they'll be talking about that day.

You may be limiting your potential audience, and it is possible that the turnout for a themed unconference will be smaller than for a general unconference, but the people who do come are likely to be passionate about the topic. Either they will already be expert practitioners who want to share their expertise, or they will be newcomers who are ready to learn and ask questions.

A themed library camp may lead more directly to action. Several of the themed camps mentioned in the earlier examples featured sessions (usually toward the end of the day) where participants stopped talking about libraries and started *doing* something for libraries, right there as part of the unconference. There is much more potential for this move from brainstorming to action and implementation when everyone is working on similar projects.

One aspect of the more general library camp that is likely to be lost in a themed event is the diversity of viewpoints that come from librarians working in different kinds of libraries and in different kinds of jobs. That is a trade-off that you may be quite willing to make, but that cross-pollination is a considerable benefit of the wide-open library camp.

Keynote Sessions

The group-driven breakout sessions are usually the heart of the unconference, but that doesn't mean that a library camp cannot feature a keynote speaker or other preplanned talks. Keynote speeches are usually high-level thought pieces rather than research reports or a "how we done it good" talk about a particular library's experience, and they can be a good way to kick off your event. Keynote speakers are usually people who have built up a name for themselves in the profession and are widely acknowledged to be good public speakers who bring some authority and experience to their talk. A good keynote speech can get library campers thinking and talking about the issues raised in the speech right away. The mere presence on the preliminary schedule of a keynote speaker with a recognizable name—a prominent blogger or columnist, perhaps—can attract attendees to the library camp.

If you invite a keynote speaker, make sure to keep communication channels open. You need to communicate what you want out of the keynote session, and you also need to make sure that you meet the speaker's needs when it comes to things like the audio/visual setup. David Lee King, the Digital Branch & Services Manager at the Topeka & Shawnee County Public Library, is a frequent speaker at library conferences and staff development days. King was a keynote speaker at the Allen County (Indiana) Public Library Camp in 2008, and in a telephone interview (March 26, 2009), he underlined the need for communication: "Some conferences communicate a lot ahead of time and others hardly do at all; I just know that I'm supposed to be there at two o'clock. If you are going to invite someone, take the time to think things through and communicate."

King said he felt that one of the great strengths of having a keynote for an unconference is the amount of cohesion it can bring to the event. "A keynote works well when you design a whole day around the topic. The talk can give a good start to the day and get everyone thinking along the same lines." John Blyberg made the same point about the speakers he brought in for a keynote and plenary session at the Not-Quite-Summit on the Future of Libraries held at the Darien Public Library in March 2009: "I had a very specific focus for the day in my mind, which was a departure from past events I'd done where 'whatever happened, happened.' And having John Berry speak about our duty as librarians really set the tone for the day."

As David Lee King pointed out, if you want that perfect setup, robust communication is key: "If you have a specific goal in mind for the day, you need to say 'here is our plan, can you do this?' Otherwise the speaker may just do his usual thing."

You also need to be prepared to talk about compensation. Engaging a keynote speaker may have an impact on your budget. Composing and delivering a 45-minute or hour-long speech is *work*, and many people may not be willing to do it without being paid. If you are looking for a speaker beyond your immediate area—which is something you might have to do if you are looking for someone with name recognition—you will also have to factor in transportation costs, lodging, and other expenses. It is only reasonable for invited keynote speakers to expect this kind of consideration. Be prepared to discuss payment and accommodation. If you can't pay (or can't pay much), that's fine, but expect that many potential speakers will decline your invitation.

Pecha Kucha Sessions and Lightning Talks

Besides keynote speeches, there are other kinds of sessions that require advance planning. Pecha kucha is an increasingly popular type of session. According to Momus (2006), "Pecha kucha—pronounced *pet-shah coot-shah*—is an onomatopoeic Japanese phrase meaning 'the sound of casual chatter.'" Participants present 20 slides (using PowerPoint or a similar presentation program). They are allowed only 20 seconds for each slide, resulting in a 6-minute and 40-second presentation for each participant. It forces people to be creative and get right to the point. Sometimes pecha kucha is set up as a contest, with a winner determined by audience applause. Pecha kucha can fit in well with an unconference because it is fast, fun, and does not allow any one person to hog the stage for more than seven minutes. It should be obvious, however, that pecha kucha presentations require preparation. At the very least, the presenter must compose 20 relevant slides in advance—and presenters would need to be arranged before the start of the unconference.

Lightning talks are similar to pecha kucha in that they put a strict time limit on the presenter—usually five minutes—but lack the other formal restrictions of the pecha kucha. Lightning talks can be arranged in advance (to allow speakers to rehearse and prepare slides or other visuals) or can be less formal, with a set number of slots available to the first people at the library camp who volunteer to fill them. As with pecha kucha, a strict time-keeper is necessary lest the lighting talks end up rambling on.

Preplanned Sessions and Open Space

It is best to lead off with keynotes and more structured sessions as the first thing on the day's schedule. Library campers will find it jarring if they are jumping back and forth between open, participant-driven sessions and more structured or traditional sessions. Harrison Owen, the originator of Open Space Technology (see the Introduction to this book) says that there is one fundamental principle to keep in mind when combining Open Space activities with other activities: "*Never interrupt Open Space with something else. When you are doing Open Space, do it. When it is over, it is over*" (Owen, 2008: 36, emphasis in original). According to Owen, participants will have no trouble if the structured part of the program comes before the Open Space discussions, but when a keynote or other similar event follows Open Space, "experience has shown that the results are less than optimal. The level of synergy and creativity is typically so high in Open Space that it is difficult to sit still and listen to a speaker at the conclusion, even a very exciting speaker" (Owen, 2008: 37).

If you are going to have preplanned sessions, think about what that says about the "open" nature of your event. Regardless of whatever else makes your library camp unique, one thing that you know will set it apart from typical library conferences is the unstructured, informal, unconference-ness of it all. Do you want to sacrifice some of that spontaneity? On his blog Overdue Ideas, Owen Stephens wrote about his experience organizing Mashed Libraries UK 2008. The schedule for that event featured planned presentations in the morning, with more Open Space–style activities in the afternoon. Writing about the morning's invited talks, Stephens says, "What surprised me (but perhaps was not really surprising) was the extent to which these presentations set the agenda for the day—people tended to look at the stuff covered in these presentations. This isn't a bad thing at all, but worth noting when planning this kind of event" (Stephens, 2008).

Your planned speakers will have an outsized impact on the event's participants' ideas of what they should be talking about at library camp. If the great strength of a library camp is its lack of hierarchy and the equality of its participants' voices, you should think carefully about upsetting that balance with a keynote speaker or other planned presentations.

▶ PROVIDE EQUIPMENT, SUPPLIES, AND SERVICES

Library camps and unconferences are primarily about getting people together to share and discuss ideas. It is tempting to say that you don't really need any equipment beyond a space with some tables and chairs to have an unconference (and if you are going to get overly literal about "library camp," you could have it in the woods, sitting on blankets under trees and dispense with even the tables and chairs), but in most cases unconferences need some equipment, supplies, and services if they are to function smoothly.

While people and the ideas they bring with them are the core of the event, people tend to be more productive if they have some support in the form of tools to work with. Participants may need projectors or whiteboards to illustrate their ideas or flip charts to document their brainstorming sessions. They may want to demonstrate software or Web sites that will demand an Internet connection. In a day-long event people will need food and drink multiple times, and it is a friendly touch to give participants a small gift to say "thank you for coming."

Consistency

It will save you some time and worry if every breakout room has the same equipment. At the Library Camp of the West, we had most of our rooms set up with a laptop and a portable projector, along with a flip chart and markers. We also had two classrooms in the library, one with a computer for each participant and the other with an instructor's computer and projector and screen.

If you can't provide a certain baseline setup for each room, you will need to note on the master schedule what each room has so that you can assign rooms accordingly when making the schedule. You may need to institute a kind of "use it or lose it" ethic, where people can improvise a Law of Two Hands whereby they can feel free to grab a flip chart or a projector from a room where they aren't being used. Doing so, however, will make it a bit more difficult to take inventory at the end of the day to be sure that all the equipment you borrowed gets back to its rightful owner.

Whiteboards and Flip Charts

The emphasis at an unconference isn't on carefully crafted presentations and PowerPoint slides, but people will still need the means to get their ideas across to a room full of people. Whiteboards (like chalkboards for dry-erase markers) are popular tools, and if your facility has whiteboards already installed, so much the better. In that case, you need to just ensure that each room has a small assortment of colored whiteboard markers and an eraser, and things are ready to go.

If the facility doesn't have whiteboards built in, don't worry about it. They are too heavy and unwieldy to bring to the site yourself. Instead, bring a flip chart or easel pad for each room, along with colored markers for each pad. Most of these oversized paper tablets need an easel to support them, but you can also find flip charts with cardboard covers that unfold to create their own desktop stand. These will be the most versatile, so if you have to spend part of your budget on flip charts, go for the self-supporting ones.

Laptops and Projectors

If you can swing it, it is nice to provide projectors, perhaps with dedicated laptops, in your breakout rooms. Unlike more traditional conferences, it's unlikely that most of the people who want to speak at the unconference will have a PowerPoint presentation to give, but with more and more library work mediated by technology, it's just about certain that some participants will want to show a document or a Web site as part of the discussion. Even when technology is not the focus of the session, participants can use a laptop and a projector to show the library camp wiki or to take notes in a format that all the participants can see as they are being written.

While library camp participants will depend on you to arrange for projectors rather than bringing projectors themselves, it's more and more likely that a significant number of attendees will bring laptops. If the focus of your unconference is technology, the likelihood increases. So if you want to offer projection in your breakout rooms, it's much more important to line up the projectors than the laptops. The advantage to providing the laptops is that you can hook them up at the beginning of the day, test them, and feel confident that they will work for the rest of the event. If people really want to use their own computers, it is a simple operation to swap their laptop for the one you have provided.

Wireless Internet

Wireless Internet connections are becoming a standard feature of traditional library conferences, and you can expect that unconference participants will want connectivity, too. Unless your event skews heavily to the tech savvy, the percentage of people at the library camp who want wireless access will be relatively small. But the people who do want it are likely to *really* want it, and perhaps even be depending on that access for their contribution to the event. I recommend that you make it clear on the event wiki whether you are going to have wireless access or not so that there are no surprises.

How you provide that access will vary based on the site's policy. Chances are you won't be setting up wireless access using your own hardware (and if you are, then I salute you; configuring wireless networks is beyond the scope of this book). Instead, you'll need to talk carefully and in some detail with the information technology staff at the site. Some sites, such as public libraries, may provide quite easy wireless access if they are already set up for public use. Academic sites typically limit access to students and employees and will require more forethought and planning for you to get access for your participants. Even public libraries may require the user to get a login or enter a library card number (which your attendees are unlikely to have), so be sure you have this squared away well in advance. Get it in writing and check the fine print: at the ALA

Unconference in 2009, the wireless network allowed only a small number of simultaneous connections, frustrating the attendees who weren't the first to get logged on that morning.

At the Library Camp of the West, we arranged in advance for a block of one-day logins to the university's wireless network. We had several dozen of these logins and ended up handing out a small fraction of them to participants. We had some trouble with the temporary logins not working at the start of the day. Some of the librarians from the host institution helped out by letting people use their computers—where they had logged on with their personal account—until we could get the temporary logins working properly.

Food and Drink

You need to have some plan to get people fed multiple times during the day. That doesn't mean that you have to cater your entire event; it just means that you need to plan appropriate breaks (as you did when creating your outline schedule as we discussed earlier) and make sure that food is available at the site or nearby.

Lunch will the biggest thing you have to consider when it comes to food. Different events have handled this differently in the past. Some unconference organizers feel that to have participants "on their own" for lunch runs the risk of having the event lose steam after lunch. According to Kathryn Greenhill and Constance Wiebrands (2008), "For the Western Australian library unconferences, we decided to provide lunch although the venue was in the middle of the restaurant district. We felt that it was important to keep the group together to continue the momentum of the day and to allow informal networking" (see Figure 2.8).

At the Library Camp of the West, we took the opposite approach and made no set arrangements for lunch. Rather than try to arrange a catered lunch or to do things on the cheap with pizza delivery or the like, we thought that participants would appreciate the opportunity to find a lunch option that would suit them and either carry on the morning's discussions over lunch or treat it as a solely social time. The venue, the University of Denver, is close to many affordable restaurants, and one of the organizers, Joe Kraus, took

▶ Figure 2.8: Pizza for Library 2.0 on the Loose Unconference, Perth 2007 (Photo by Kathryn Greenhill; www.flickr.com/ photos/sirexkat/1001327061/)

the time to put together a wiki page with a Google Map and list of the restaurants in the area, so out-of-towners could easily find a place that suited them. Another advantage of leaving it to participants to find their own lunch is that you don't need to worry about special diets, food allergies, and so on (e.g., the vegans aren't going to be real happy with that cheese pizza you ordered for the vegetarians). The downside is that no matter how long you schedule for lunch (we allowed 90 minutes), when left to their own devices some people will inevitably straggle back on the late side.

In addition to lunch, people will likely need some other breaks with food in the morning and afternoon. There is plenty of room for flexibility here. You can have breakfast food available at check-in so that people can eat a bit as they wait for the event to start or even during the opening session. Or you can choose to have a more organized midmorning coffee break. Unless you are ending in the midafternoon, you will probably also want to schedule a break in the afternoon as well.

Harrison Owen suggests a plan for refreshments that allows participants to fuel up on their own schedule, without needing to fit snacks into a scheduled break. "For example," writes Owen, "all meals can be served as buffets over a several-hour period, allowing people to come and go as they please. For coffee breaks, try replacing the fifteen-minute mad dash, which nobody observes anyhow, with a more leisurely approach. The world will not come to an end if the beverages and snacks are left out for an hour or longer" (Owen, 2008: 40).

Regardless, remember that while it's important to make sure people get a chance to eat, no one comes to an unconference for the food. Give people a few opportunities to eat, make it very clear on the wiki what the participants can expect, and don't worry about it anymore.

Where to Get Your Supplies

Use the resources of your chosen site. Once you have an idea of what you need, make sure to ask your hosts what they can provide. Even if you have a tour of the site and can see what is available, it is best to ask specific questions and get specific assurances. It is great if they are providing a room with a projector and an instructor's computer, but will you be able to power it up and log in on the day of the event? Maybe there are no whiteboards in sight, but, if you ask, you may find that they will get some out of the storage closet for you.

Anything dealing with technology adds another layer of possible difficulty, as there are more chances for things to malfunction, passwords to keep track of, and so on. Be sure to have a local technology contact for any technology equipment or services (see Chapter 3 for more on troubleshooting on the day of the event).

Beg or borrow the supplies (librarians don't *steal*, we just return things very overdue). Don't forget that the library camp participants are responsible for the success of the event just as much as you are. If the host institution doesn't have a half-dozen data projectors handy, try asking for volunteers via the wiki or e-mail list. It may be more realistic to find six attendees from different institutions who could each bring one projector for the day than to expect the host to provide everything. When it comes to less-valuable items like flip charts and markers, most libraries will have a few of them stuffed away in a supply closet, untouched since that last vision statement planning retreat five years ago.

Create a master list of everything you borrow. You will have so many things to think about on the day of the event, you won't remember who volunteered to bring what items, and, once the items are there, you won't remember who they belong to. It doesn't matter too much if your list is written in pencil or typed into a spreadsheet. Check items off your list as they arrive and as they leave. If you are borrowing a lot of material before the event that you are transporting to and from the site, you may want to check them off once as you load them out after the event is over and again after you finally return them to where they belong. On the day of the event, keep a roll of masking tape and a marker with you (or a portable label printer if you have one), and label everything in your care so that you can easily recognize it and get it back to its owner.

Souvenirs or Schwag

The last of the amenities you need to plan for is optional, but recommended. It's a souvenir or giveaway or "schwag." People shouldn't expect to get a gift for attending the event, but if you can provide a small giveaway, imprinted with the name or logo of your unconference, so much the better. If you have gone to the trouble to create or commission a logo or illustration for your event, you will especially want to have a place to immortalize it. People are delighted with gifts, even small ones, and a giveaway makes people feel a bit more like they are part of a fun, special day. Besides, most conferences have speakers' gifts, and at library camp everyone is a speaker. Let them know you appreciate their contribution.

T-shirts are an obvious choice for a souvenir and seem to be the standard item at technology conferences. Consider, however, that if you are going to give away T-shirts, you will have to have a registration process that allows people to choose a shirt size, and you will have to make sure that people get the proper size shirt when they register. That's not an insurmountable difficulty, of course, but it is a small added layer of complexity when you have to match people up with shirt sizes.

Instead, it is easier to have a giveaway that doesn't have to be customized per person. At Library Camp East and Library Camp of the West, the souvenir was a coffee mug (see Figure 2.9), and at the 2007 Library Camp NYC they gave away little notebooks with the Manhattan skyline and the name of the event printed on the cover. The "#unala2009" buttons that sported the hashtag for the 2009 ALA Unconference were simple and inexpensive but still a fun giveaway that people could wear throughout the conference (see Figure 2.10).

▶ Figure 2.9: Library Camp of the West 2008 Mug (Photo by Joe Kraus; www.flickr
.com/photos/jokrausdu/2894140670/)

▶ Figure 2.10: ALA Unconference 2009 Buttons (Photo by Michelle Boule; www.flickr
.com/photos/wanderingeyre/3697363561/)

Sample List of Supplies and Equipment

As you work through the details of your library camp, compile a list of
all the supplies and equipment you will need. Here is a sample list:

- ▶ Duct tape
- ▶ Easel pads/flip charts and markers
- ▶ Extension cords and surge protectors
- ▶ First-aid kit
- ▶ Laptops
- ▶ Masking tape
- ▶ Nametags (create-your-own is much easier than preprinted)
- ▶ Projectors
- ▶ Souvenirs
- ▶ Sticky notes (various sizes, including 3 × 5 if you can)
- ▶ Whiteboards, markers, and erasers

▶ DETERMINE YOUR BUDGET AND FUNDING SOURCES

Unconferences are often free as in "someone else is paying for it." That's a fine attitude for most of the participants to take, but as an unconference organizer you can't afford to be ignorant about where the money is coming from and where it is going. In this section, we'll look at the typical expenses for a library camp and examine a few ways to pay for those expenses.

Expenses

The main categories of expenses break down like this:

- ▶ Space
- ▶ Food
- ▶ Supplies
- ▶ Souvenirs/schwag
- ▶ Invited guests (speaker's fees, transportation, etc.)

The good news is that you have some degree of control over all of these categories, and some of these categories (schwag and guests) you need not worry about at all if you are trying to do things as inexpensively as possible.

Space Rental

You may not need to pay for space. If you have a library or other host organization that controls its own space, you might simply need a director or other person in charge to grant you use of the space for your event. If you end up having to look elsewhere for space, such as in a university conference center or student center, or a community space, it's more likely that you will have to pay. In that case, count on the space rental being a significant percentage of your budget.

For Library Camp of the West 2008, we paid about $600.00 for the use of one ballroom and five smaller meeting rooms for one day. It is hard to say if that is a typical figure, and had the event not been sponsored by the Library and Information Science Program at the University, it's possible that we would have paid much more.

Food

Preparing snacks on your own will certainly be cheaper but will add more work and logistical coordination. Using a caterer will cost significantly more but will mean that once you have paid for their services you will not have to worry about the food and beverage service at all.

Supplies

When it comes to nametags, markers, flip charts, and other office supplies, do your best to scavenge those from the supply closets of the organizations you are working with. Many of these things won't be fully used up during the event, so, unless your institution has unusually strict guidelines for using office supplies, you will be able to return most items you borrow almost as good as new.

Souvenirs/Schwag

Of course souvenirs is an area where there is a lot of variation and where you need not buy anything at all if you don't have the sponsorship. Be aware if you are ordering from a large promotional products supplier that shipping and setup charges can be a significant part of the total cost, especially if the items you choose are large or heavy. You may also have to order a certain minimum number or order in cases of 36 or some such number. For Library Camp of the West 2008, we paid about $550.00 to have 216 mugs imprinted with our design and delivered. On the other side of the spectrum, Michelle Boule paid about $30.00 for buttons for the first ALA Unconference in 2009.

Invited Guests

The budget for guests all depends on who you get, what their rate is, and whether you need to pay for transportation, food and lodging, and so on. A local expert might ask for no compensation, and you can get away with a $20.00 gift card as a thank-you. A "big name" (if there are such things in libraryland) flying in from out of state can command a substantial fee on top of the transportation costs. If you decide to try and bring in a known speaker, have a budget before you talk to her, lest you have someone wonderful all lined up with only a fraction of the money you need.

Sponsors

For some library camps, the sole sponsor is the host library. John Blyberg has put on numerous library camps and similar events, and each time the Darien Public Library has hosted and paid for everything. Darien is often thought of as a wealthy library, but, in our phone interview, Blyberg put it simply in terms of the value to the library: "It's actually much more cost-effective to bring eighty people here and feed them lunch than it is to send one person to a conference and pay for that one person's hotel, airfare, and food. This way the whole staff can participate, and we get a lot more bang for the buck."

If your institution has the space to pull it off, this argument of the value to the library staff is a compelling place to start if you need to try to convince a higher-up that hosting an unconference is a good idea. Another possible argument is that you can raise your library's profile in the library community or the community at large. Hosting an unconference will make your library stand out as a place that is interested in innovation and fostering discussion about libraries. In Halifax, Nova Scotia, the Halifax Public Libraries hosted PodCamp Halifax, a BarCamp-style meeting about social media. Ryan Deschamps, e-Learning Services Manager at Halifax, said that by hosting the PodCamp, the library gained a great deal of favorable press and notoriety: "I got my face pasted on a whole bunch of community newspapers. We had a television segment where I was being asked about why people use social media. So all of a sudden the library is set up where I'm an expert in social media and why people use it, which is a good fit for libraries. Participants said 'oh, I didn't realize I could use the library in this way'" (interview May 4, 2009).

But if your library can't afford to foot the entire bill, or if your boss still isn't sold on it, you can still find sponsors to help with the bottom line. About half of Library Camp of the West 2008 was financed by the University of Denver Library and Information Science Program and University of Denver Penrose Library, while the other half was financed by sponsors.

Don't be shy about approaching vendors. The smallest booth at the ALA Annual Meeting Exhibits costs close to $2,000.00 to rent. For one-tenth of that cost they could be a major sponsor of your event. Think regionally when you are brainstorming what groups or vendors to approach. Sponsors of Library Camp of the West 2008 paid from $100.00 to $250.00 to sponsor the event, and most of that came from local companies and organizations.

Have some of your costs in mind when you approach possible sponsors. If you know that food is likely to run $500.00 or the souvenirs between $200.00 and $400.00 then you will be able to hold that out to vendors or groups. Perhaps if they paid for the souvenirs there would be room for their logo somewhere? If they paid for the food, they could send promotional materials to put out at the time of the meal.

Some people may object to a camp sponsored in this way, preferring only the most homemade of unconferences. But if you work with local vendors and groups, and you invite them to send promotional materials or staff a table and also be part of the actual conversations in the breakout rooms, you are doing something to foster community throughout libraryland.

Registration Fees

In general, I am against charging participants in library camps a registration fee. I'm against it philosophically because I think it sends the wrong message. It sets up a customer/service provider relationship between the participants and the organizers. It can lead to participants thinking "are the organizers giving me my money's worth?" rather than "am I fully participating in making this event a success?" Registration fees contribute to the divide between those who have institutional funding for conferences and

Tips for Talking to Potential Sponsors

Don't sell yourself short. Five hundred dollars, for example, seems like big money when you think about paying it out of your own pocket. But for a vendor or a library that likely has a budget for public relations or promotional activities, it could seem very reasonable. Start with a figure that seems a little high, and then be willing to scale back from there.

Money is just one thing they can donate. Don't get too hung up on money. A sponsor who can donate items like food, flip charts, or souvenirs; equipment such as projectors and laptops; or services like photocopying or printing can be just as valuable as a cash sponsor.

What's in it for them? You are likely to be thinking about how important the money is to your event, but that can't be the only thing you talk to your sponsors about. Yes, to some degree they are giving money to be nice, but they will certainly want to know what they will get for their donation. Corporate sponsors would probably be happy with a link and a logo on your wiki and a seat at a vendor table, if you have room for such a thing. Mugs, T-shirts, and other giveaways can easily carry sponsors' logos. Institutional sponsors may simply want to be associated with a forward-thinking event such as yours, and a photo and a blurb for their "news and events" Web page might be enough. Libraries who sponsor are also likely to want to have a few guaranteed registration spots for their staff or a waiver of some fees if you are charging them.

professional development and those who don't. It ignores the fact that participants are already making an investment of time, transportation costs, and perhaps a vacation day or two in order to attend the event.

Still, there are valid reasons for asking participants to pay to register. If community responsibility is a big part of the unconference, shouldn't the community shoulder some of the cost? It is easy to just sign up on a wiki to "register" for an unconference when there is no fee, so it is hard to judge whether those who registered are really planning to attend. What some people call a "nuisance fee" of $20.00 to $40.00 may deter people from signing up, but perhaps it only deters those who aren't really all that interested in attending in the first place.

These considerations aside, I'm against registration fees for practical reasons, too. When you can put on an entire one-day conference for between $1,000.00 and $3,000.00, it just seems easier to try to raise that money hundreds of dollars at a time from sponsors than in small amounts from every single participant.

▶3

IMPLEMENTATION

- ▶ Prepare the Conference Location
- ▶ Create the Schedule
- ▶ Suggest Procedures for Breaking Out
- ▶ Understand When and How to Fix Problems
- ▶ Break Camp and Follow Up

▶ PREPARE THE CONFERENCE LOCATION

The morning of your event is likely to be a bit hectic. It is exciting to have the day you have been planning for finally arrive. If you are nervous, that's only natural. Don't worry too much. Even John Blyberg, who has organized many such events, said in a telephone interview (May 4, 2009) that he still gets nervous before an event. "I still get nervous about people spending their time. They are there to come away with something and if they don't, then as an organizer, I feel like I would have failed." Remember that what they take away, though, is largely up to the participants. You are just providing them the occasion and opportunity to exchange ideas. Most of what they take away is up to them.

To provide the best possible opportunity to the participants, you will need to spend some time setting up before the event begins. This chapter will run down some of the things you should do or think about in those final hours. Much of this is common sense, but if you think about it ahead of time and perhaps even make a checklist, you can be more confident that you will actually get everything done in a timely manner before the first session.

Showing Up

There's more to this than just showing up, but getting there and getting there early is important. Aim to be on site at least an hour before the first time stated on your preliminary schedule. So, if you scheduled coffee, donuts, and registration from 8:00 to 9:00 a.m., plan to be there by 7:00 a.m. If you are bringing a lot of equipment and supplies on the day of the event, it could take you a significant amount of time just to unpack the car.

Examining the Site

The first thing to do is examine your site. If the site is your usual place of work, this might not take very long, but if you are working with another library or organization that provided the space, make sure to leave yourself time to be fairly thorough. Do you have all the rooms you were promised? Are tables and chairs set up in an agreed upon fashion, or is it up to you to set them up? Locate the closest bathrooms, as we all know from reference desk shifts that "where is the bathroom?" is likely to be a frequently asked question.

Setting Up Registration

Most of the time, "registration" at an unconference is a pretty informal affair. People show up, maybe get their name checked off a list, write their name on a nametag, grab some printed materials for the day (blank schedule form, map, list of restaurants, etc.) or the conference souvenir, and then head off to look for coffee. If your event is more formal, perhaps with a registration fee, you may need to make registration more formal as well by checking IDs against your registration list or taking money from late registrants.

Get the registration table set up as soon as you can after examining your site. You don't necessarily have to station anyone to sit there until closer to the actual time you said registration would begin, but having an obvious registration desk, clearly marked as such with the name of your event (and your logo if you have one) will let early-birds know that they are in the right place and establish a base for participants to congregate around.

As you get closer to the stated registration time, have someone posted at the desk to greet people and help them register. This could be you or other members of the planning team, but if you anticipate a lot of work setting up the site, it's probably better to just get a volunteer so people more familiar with the plans for the day can be available to set up and troubleshoot.

Preparing Food

Make sure that preparations for food are in place as you have planned them, especially if you have arranged for coffee or breakfast early in the day. If you are working with a catering company or campus food service or the like, talk to them as they are setting up and make sure they have the meals or breaks on their schedule the way you expect it. If volunteers are bringing and preparing food, make sure they have ample space to work that is clean and safe.

Setting Up the Rooms

After your quick examination of the site, you will need to spend some more time in all of the rooms to get them ready. In cases where you have a lot of breakout rooms, do your best to get other organizers or volunteers to help out. If the tables and chairs aren't already set up to your liking, you may spend some time doing that, or simply mention in the opening session that breakout groups will want to rearrange the rooms. Any supplies that you brought for the breakout rooms, such as flip charts, markers, scratch paper, and sticky notes, should be distributed at this time.

If you are working with technology in each room, set up and test it now. For equipment supplied by the host, such as computers or projectors in a lab, make sure you are able to log on and get Internet access (assuming that is part of the agreement you worked out ahead of time), and if you can't, start trying to reach your site technical contact as soon as possible. For equipment that you and other volunteers are providing, make sure it is clearly labeled with a personal name or organization's name, and get it set up and tested as well.

Testing the Wireless Internet Connection

Wireless can be one of the biggest headaches if it doesn't work properly. As soon as you can, try out the wireless access using a laptop that hasn't ever used that network before—a laptop from the host institution may have an easier time getting on than someone from outside. If you can get on the network, be cautiously optimistic. If you can't, start working with other organizers or volunteers from the host site immediately, and start trying to contact your local technical support as soon as possible (recognizing that they might very well not be at work at 7:30 a.m.).

Making Sponsors and Vendors Comfortable

If your event is sponsored by vendors and you have made arrangements for some kind of display space, make sure the vendor area is set up properly with the correct numbers of tables and chairs and so on. Have someone keep an eye out for the vendors as they arrive and help them get situated at their table. Make sure to thank them for their sponsorship, and remind them that they are welcome to take part in as much of the unconference as they desire, as long as they can resist putting on a hard sell during sessions.

Getting Ready for the First Session

If, as I recommend, you are starting the day with an all-group session either to create the final schedule or just to make some announcements and get people going, you will need to prepare the large meeting room for that session. If you are using a computer and projector, get that all warmed up and ready to go. If you are using a flip chart and sticky notes, or Open Space–style index cards, make sure those are handy and ready to go.

▶ CREATE THE SCHEDULE

After your welcome and opening announcements, the first order of the day is to create the schedule. It may sound like a daunting task—you have to take a roomful of people, solicit their ideas, and create a schedule that everyone is happy with (or at least that everyone can live with). But with a bit of forethought and planning, the scheduling session can become a model for your entire day. The scheduling involves participation, discussion, compromise, and patience, all of which are qualities and themes that will run throughout your library camp.

It may seem like a bad idea to set the schedule on the day of the event. Some of your library campers will find it inefficient and strange and wish that things had been set up beforehand. But creating the schedule in a collaborative manner with the people who actually attend the library camp—not the people who wanted to attend or thought they possibly could attend, but the people who are actually there and ready to work—is a signature event of the unconference.

Setting the Tone

It is important that you set the tone for your day when you create the schedule. You need to create the right combination of excitement and fun on the one hand and serious work on the other. You need to reassure those attendees who crave structure that the day will not be complete anarchy while also signaling to the attendees who are excited by the freedom of the unconference that the content and structure of the day is still in the hands of the entire group and not just a cabal of conference organizers. It is a balancing act, but it is also simply a continuation of what you have already been doing on the conference wiki and e-mail list.

Another message you are likely to be sending is that the day will not flow perfectly, and that is just fine. There is likely to be some confusion during the scheduling. People will suggest ideas that very few others are interested in. People will disagree as to whether two related topics should be combined or remain as separate sessions. People will complain that the scheduling isn't efficient or that there are too many related topics scheduled opposite one another.

But if you handle all that with thoughtful good humor, and throw problems back to the group to decide instead of making arbitrary decisions yourself, the campers will trust the process and own the unconference as their collaborative creation.

Turning Ideas into Sessions

You should have a list of suggested topics that campers have posted to the camp wiki. Depending on how enthusiastically the attendees have taken to the task, you may have a list of dozens of very specific ideas or just a short list of general topics. This list will provide you with a valuable jump-start for your schedule. If the list is coherent enough, or if your camp has a theme, you may be able to decide on a few "tracks" or groups of related sessions ahead of time.

Instead of taking those ideas from the camp wiki as a given, you will want to read them out and remind people of what they have already suggested that they would like to talk about. After everyone has heard the list, it is time to get people to speak up and take ownership of the various sessions. You can start by simply asking, "who has heard something on that list that they would like to turn into a session today?" When someone speaks up, make it clear that he or she has now agreed to be a moderator or speaker in that session, and record that session topic.

There are many conceivable ways of physically making that list, including on paper (see Figure 3.1), a whiteboard, or a computer, but simply writing the session title on a large sticky note might be the simplest and most effective way. Sticky notes are useful because you can put one session per note, and then easily arrange and repeatedly rearrange those notes on a large schedule grid (see Figure 3.2). Other erasable methods like a whiteboard or using the camp wiki are perfectly acceptable but may involve more erasing and rewriting or typing than you really want to do.

▶ Figure 3.1: Partial Session Schedule for Library Camp Kansas 2009 (Photo by KathrynGreenhill; www.flickr.com/photos/sirexkat/3365007799/)

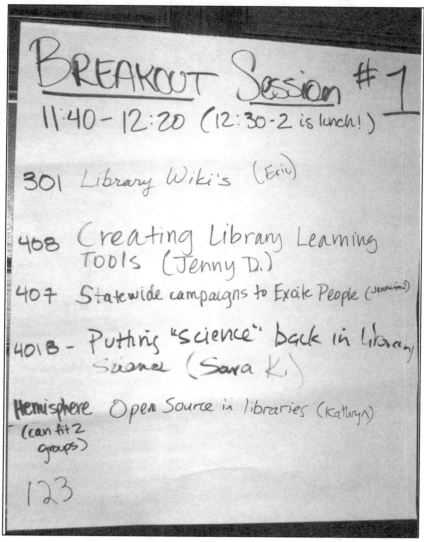

As you write down the proposed sessions, be patient and take your time. You and the campers will be excited and will want to get past the schedule and on to the real business of the day. But it is important to get the schedule done calmly and correctly.

▶ Figure 3.2: Library Camp of the West 2008 Schedule

Keep an eye out for sessions that you can combine, especially if it seems likely that you will have more suggested sessions than you have time slots available. There is no need to be arbitrary or authoritarian when combining sessions. Put the question back to the group: "Do these two sessions belong together? Can we have a better discussion if we combine these? Are the people who are interested in subject X the same people who want to discuss subject Y?" You don't need to press the issue if campers resist (it is their conference, after all), but be aware of those possibilities and mindful of the fact that if you have more suggested sessions than you have time slots, some of those sessions will have to combine or perish.

Last, be open and do not judge the suggestions as they come in. It is quite likely that some of the ideas suggested will be ones that you think are poorly conceived, done to death elsewhere, or simply inexplicable. This isn't the time to try to shoot them down. You may be surprised how many campers want to discuss that "bad" idea. Or, if it turns out that very few people are interested, you can tactfully suggest folding that idea into a related, more popular session. Like a brainstorming session, this is the time to say "yes" to every idea, knowing that some ideas will have to change if they are to fit into the eventual full schedule with room assignments.

Turning Sessions into a Schedule

A list of sessions is still not a schedule. They need to be assigned specific points in space and time before you can call it a schedule.

In your planning process, you have already set the number of rooms that you have available to you, and you have noted the capacity for each of those rooms. You have also already come up with a skeleton of a schedule, so you know how many breakout sessions you have planned for the day. Using that information, you can create a grid, listing your breakout rooms down the left side and the breakout sessions and times across the top.

This grid gives you the visual outline of the time and space you have available for your breakout sessions. You'll want to have that grid large enough so that participants can see it. For smaller rooms, a whiteboard or a flip chart will be just fine and will work well with the sticky notes that list the sessions. If you have a larger room and a projector handy, you might want to use a blank text document or a page of the conference wiki to display the schedule-in-progress.

Because attendees won't have the benefit of a preprinted schedule, it might be wise to give them their own grid to fill out (see Figure 3.3). If the camp is fairly small with a small number of breakout sessions, it might be enough to have the schedule on a whiteboard in the main meeting room. If group members are all using laptops and wireless devices, they'll be fine with having the schedule on the conference wiki. In many situations, though, your attendees will be happy to have a simple grid of their own to fill out so that they can plan their day and know where else they might want to be when they choose to exercise the Law of Two Feet.

To assign the rooms, you will need an idea of how many people want to attend each session. This information will help you in several ways:

▶ Figure 3.3: Blank Schedule (Photo by Nicole C. Engard; www.flickr.com/photos/ nengard/1116350120/)

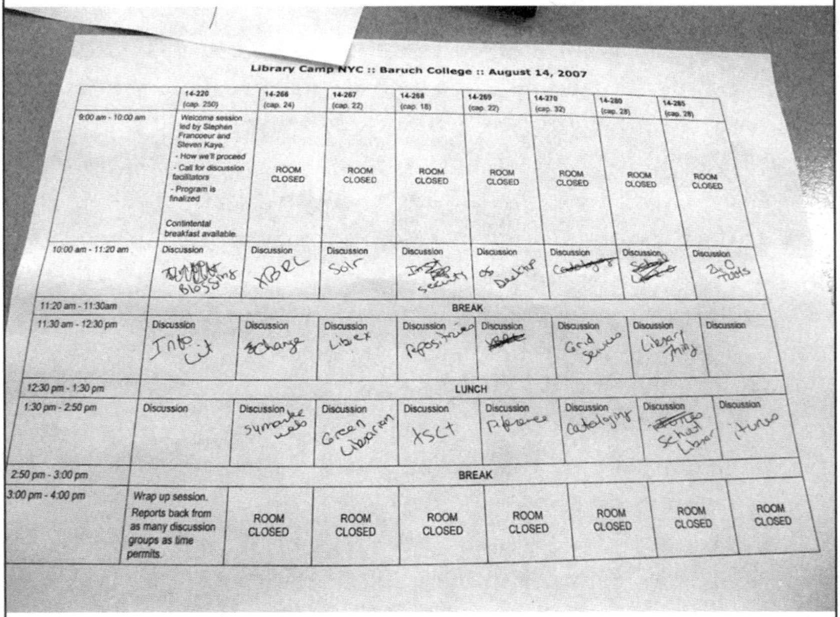

- ▶ You can avoid scheduling the most popular sessions opposite one another.
- ▶ When you have more suggested topics that you have time slots, you can eliminate the less-popular topics.
- ▶ If you have rooms of varying capacity, you can assign sessions to rooms appropriately.

How you take your head count will vary by the type and size of the conference. For the Library Camp of the West, we just asked people to raise their hands if they thought they were likely to attend a given session, and we got a rough impression of how popular the session was likely to be. If you feel you need to be more precise, or if you have many more sessions than you have slots and want to be as fair as possible in determining which sessions get cut, you can do a more exact count by posting all the sessions around the room or on one wall or whiteboard and asking people to put hash marks or colored stickers under no more than a certain number of sessions, as in "choose your top five."

You may not want to schedule every available room for every breakout session. For the Library Camp of the West, we had a large ballroom for our central meeting place and a small room with food and the vendor tables that we intended to keep unscheduled to allow for small, informal groups to congregate. We did end up scheduling one session in the ballroom when it wasn't clear if we had one cohesive topic or if that group would split into subgroups during the session. The ballroom was again pressed into service when it became clear that one session on "Impractical, Unfeasible, Unfundable Ideas" was so popular we wouldn't fit in the room originally assigned. If you are lucky enough to have enough space, leaving this kind of escape valve can be helpful.

It is possible that as the organizer of the library camp, you may find yourself too close to the event to create the schedule, or you might want to avoid the appearance of trying to control the entire day. You could consider asking someone to facilitate the scheduling session. But it is important that you consider this ahead of time and find the right person, as scheduling is not a place for someone who can't stay on schedule or make decisions.

▶ SUGGEST PROCEDURES FOR BREAKING OUT

This is *it*. This is what you have been planning for. This is when the people start breaking into groups and start talking about libraries. This is where it becomes obvious that it is not *your* library camp anymore: it is everybody's library camp. Whatever small degree of control you had is lost. In theory you could go off and smoke a cigarette, have a good stiff drink, or call your mom (or all three at once). In reality, you will want to stick around and be part of the whole reason you planned the day in the first place: getting people together to talk about libraries.

As you know by now, there are no rules for how a session *should* go. Small sessions will have a different feel from large sessions, technology demonstrations will not have the same feel as a small group discussion, and so on. But most sessions can benefit from a few standard procedures. You do not need to try and insist that people follow these procedures—if you have done a good job setting up a sense of shared ownership of the library camp, you will not be *able* to insist, because people will ignore you—but by suggesting certain practices, you can help ensure that the breakout sessions get off to a quick, productive start.

Introductions

Even if you were able to do introductions as part of the general opening session, encourage participants to have a round of introductions before each breakout session begins. You can think of it as networking or just common courtesy, but meeting new people and putting faces to names can be one of the best outcomes for participants in any library camp.

In addition to name and workplace and position, have people say a few words about what they are doing in this particular session. What do they want to share? What do they hope to learn? This quick round robin can give everyone present a sense of what the session will be like. Are there differing viewpoints that mean the session will end up being a debate? Are the people in the session mostly experts in the topic, or are there many people who are getting their first exposure to the ideas? No one scenario is better than any other—whoever shows up is the right group—but introductions will help everyone see where things are likely to go.

Moderators

Most sessions could profit from a moderator. Often the moderator will be the person who suggested the topic in the first place, but other times the group can easily choose a moderator with a show of hands or simply by "volunteering" someone in the group. Ideally, the moderator won't have to do very much; sometimes just starting the introductions, asking a question or making a brief statement to start the ball rolling, and watching the time to be sure the group has a chance to wrap things up in the last few minutes will be enough.

Other times, though, a moderator can keep the entire proceedings from devolving into an argument or a monolog from the most vocal member of the group. Moderators should strive to keep everyone involved, keep the discussion at least in sight of the stated topic, and keep any one person from unduly dominating the discussion.

Yes, it is an unconference, and whatever happens is the only thing that could have. But we can resist the notion that a heated argument, a single person's diatribe, or dead silence are the *only* things that could have happened.

Another simple duty of the moderator is to watch the time. In a good session, it can be easy to let the time get away from you. No one wants to cut off a productive discussion or leave something unresolved if another five minutes of discussion seems likely to wrap it up neatly. But the moderator has a responsibility to the overall schedule as well, and a session that goes over time by five minutes can have a negative effect on many of the attendees as rooms are not empty when they should be, people have less time to get to the next session, and so on.

Last, the moderator can help people make connections. When it seems that there are people in the session who have expertise and experience they could offer one another, just a simple suggestion that they exchange contact information can help them get over a social hurdle. Not all librarians are shy and retiring, of course (just ask my coworkers), but many people would appreciate a gentle nudge that gives them permission to ask for someone's business card or e-mail address. A good moderator will look for ways to help participants keep the conversation going after the library camp is over.

Notes

Encourage someone at each session to take notes. Reasonably objective minutes are a good thing, but so are the kinds of session reports we see from library bloggers. There is no reason that just one person has to take notes, either. People can provide multiple perspectives on a single session. If you have wireless for your event, people can take notes right on the conference wiki in real time (though some wikis don't allow people to collaborate in real time—the first person to start editing will effectively lock out other participants), but many times people take notes in an offline editor such as Word and upload as soon as is practical.

If the notes are visible to everyone in the breakout session, the act of taking notes becomes less of a passive secretarial duty and more of an interactive part of the session itself. A computer and a projector will work, but so will a simple flip chart. Getting people's ideas out of their heads and into a form that is visible and tangible will help people make associations. As participants see the record of the discussion forming in real time, they will be able to make connections and group certain ideas and concepts together into a larger whole. At the same time, they will be more able to see what is missing and will be motivated to participate and fill in the gaps of the conversation.

Technology

Many library camp sessions can run with little more technology than electric lights so that the participants can see one another. At the same time, if you decided to supply some level of technology for your breakout rooms such as laptops with projectors, you'll need to keep an eye on them during the sessions and make sure they are working properly (see Figure 3.4). If you are working in an institution with technology staff available, make sure you find out who is available to help and introduce yourself at the start of the day. If your conference is technology oriented, you are likely to have people capable of troubleshooting equipment among your participants, but even those people will not have much luck if they come up against local systems that require passwords.

Room Configuration

If you are meeting in a conference center or other venue where there is a staff devoted to setting up the space for you, you will likely have to decide on a room configuration beforehand. If so, you should prefer circular arrangements with chairs in a ring or "boardroom" arrangements, with everyone sitting around a central table. If you anticipate heavy use of a projector and screen, it could be more kind to set up in a horseshoe arrangement so that no one has his or her back to the screen.

▶ Figure 3.4: Library Camp of the West 2008 Breakout Session

Otherwise, as the room is filling up for the session, do not give in to inertia and let the room's existing condition dictate how you use it. Can you move the desks and chairs? Can you set the room up as a circle or horseshoe instead of classroom style with chairs or desks in rows?

When booking the rooms, it makes sense to prefer rooms with more open plans where people can all see one another and move around the room if necessary. Most of the time, your participants won't be doing "stand and deliver" lectures. It is certainly handy to have a computer lab or two to facilitate hands-on software demos or group hacking sessions, but computer labs can be deadly for conversation. Participants are looking forward at the screen rather than at one another, and computer displays get in the way when people want to talk and see one another.

► UNDERSTAND WHEN AND HOW TO FIX PROBLEMS

As long as things are running smoothly, you can fade into the group and enjoy being a participant rather than an organizer. And there is every reason to expect that things will run smoothly. With the help of this book you have put together a great plan, and, as the principles of Open Space would have it, the right people have arrived, and the only thing that could happen is happening.

But what if, despite your best efforts, things aren't going smoothly? It will be tempting for you to want to step in and get to work on any problem, no matter how small or insignificant. It is an understandable urge, but it is one that you must fight against. Part of the process of getting the unconference underway was getting all the participants to take ownership of the event and to under-stand that they were responsible for their own experience and the shared experience of the group. If you handle every little problem or request on your own, it sends the message that you are still in charge, when, in reality, the power of the group should take over.

The good news is that library camp participants are much more likely to cut you some slack when things go wrong than they would if a conference put on by a major membership organization or commercial operation were to have the exact same problems. Based on her experience with the Zine Librarians and Radical Reference unconferences, Jenna Freedman noted that "everyone is so critical about ALA, but at unconferences everyone is so appreciative of the organizers and their fellow participants" (interview, March 24, 2009). When a major conference has problems with wireless Internet access, people complain and write nasty blog posts, and say cranky things from the podium. When we had wireless trouble on the morning of the Library Camp of the West, we just had a few people politely asking us to let them know when we got the kinks out. It's like the difference between complaining about the food at a restaurant and complaining about the food at a friend's dinner party.

When people do bring problems to you, take a moment to ask yourself, "Why should I solve this problem? What would happen if I didn't try to solve this problem?" In a section titled "Empowering the People," Harrison Owen writes of an Open Space participant who was distressed at the lack of nametags at the event. Owen replied, "Great idea, why don't you take care of it?" Once the man recovered from being momentarily taken aback by Owen's response, he did take care of it. According to Owen (2008: 117–118), "the results were magnificent: in a very short time, a small group of people had answered the call of voluntary self-selection and begun to create a series of hand-painted nametags that were simply outstanding." To take things upon yourself as the organizer may seem like the responsible thing to do, but when you choose not to solve every problem you are presented with, you help participants remember that solving problems is part of the experience of the unconference. You don't want to deprive the participants of the experience of having some problem or disagreement and figuring out how to solve it on their own terms.

Instead, you should be on the lookout for problems hindering productivity, problems that really need someone to act like they are in charge. Participants are perfectly capable of coming to creative workarounds for all kinds of problems, but in the case of equipment malfunctions or problems with the venue, you, as the person whose name is on the contract, are more likely to actually get things fixed in a reasonable timeframe. Let the participants save their creative energies for more interesting problems or to find solutions when it turns out that the equipment really can't be fixed in a timely manner.

If you are going to be able to handle any problems for the participants, they will need to be able to find you. If your camp is big enough, consider stationing someone to be at the registration table at all times. You can work shifts so that there is always someone available to help (and so no one person has to spend the whole day chained to a desk). Another way of handling things is to prominently post your cell phone number, instant messaging screen name, or other contact information at the registration desk and on the library camp Web site so you can be contacted during the event, even if you are in a session or otherwise unavailable.

Venue and Equipment Problems

If the wireless access goes out or if the bulb burns out on a projector, it doesn't make sense for an entire breakout group (or the entire unconference) to stop what they are doing and try to get it fixed. In a situation like this, it's best if the participants are encouraged to carry on and do their best while you or someone else tries to get the problem actually solved.

If you are depending on the site or the venue to provide technology—wireless access, computer classrooms, smartboards, and so on—make sure you have some local tech support contact, whether it's a volunteer troubleshooter or, better, a person who works at the site whose job it is to support you. Keep that list of local contacts with you at all times. This is the kind of thing that is probably best *not* to post on the wiki. When the wireless network goes down, you don't want several dozen participants all contacting one poor IT support person. Let those participants come to you, and you can make the IT support person miserable all by yourself.

A more general-purpose site contact is a good idea, too, for less-technical questions and problems. How actually helpful those people are can vary widely. If the organization is used to supporting groups like yours, they may be very effective. But if they are used to just supporting "home" members of their institution, they may not really know what to do with you when you ask for help.

Be polite but firm with your contacts at the venue. Yelling won't help you get what you want any faster (though tears just might), but neither should you accept problems without taking them to the site's management. Sometimes, there's nothing to be done, and when you are using another library's donated space, you don't want to appear ungrateful. All the same, it is best to talk to someone who has the authority to try to make things right or to tell you that nothing can be done rather than talking to someone who may not know all the options.

If the event is sponsored by and held at your own place of work, troubleshooting can be even more fraught. You should have fewer surprises on your own turf than when working in an unfamiliar environment, and you will know who the people are who can get problems fixed. But the fact that you want the event to reflect well on your workplace might keep you from pushing some problems back on the participants to solve themselves. As always, consider first whether it might be better to just let the participants muddle through.

Even if the event isn't held at your library, don't forget to draw on the expertise of the attendees—and your fellow organizers—who do work there. At the Library Camp of the West, we found that we got more helpful, direct answers from camp participants who were also University of Denver employees than we did from the staff at the university information desk. Librarians are pathologically helpful—if they can help, they will.

If, on the other hand, the technology is of the "beg, borrow, and steal" variety, you will have to depend more on your participants. If the group in the room can't solve the problem, find the person who actually brought the laptop or the projector, or whatever the item in question is, and see if she can't get it working. If you labeled all the borrowed equipment as suggested in Chapter 2, you should not have too much trouble determining who the owner is, though finding her at that moment might be a different story.

What happens when a breakout group is assigned a room that is too small? That's the kind of problem that you, as the organizer, probably won't have to step in and solve, as the participants will be able to sort it out themselves. Several things could happen. People don't want to stand in an overcrowded room, so some of them will likely exercise the Law of Two Feet and the sessions will even out through osmosis. It's possible that a group who was assigned a larger room will have a smaller number of participants so that the two groups can just trade rooms. Last, this is a reason why it is a good idea to have a large gathering space that doesn't get scheduled for breakout rooms. In a pinch, it can absorb a large group or even multiple groups (see Figure 3.5).

People Problems

If the problem isn't with the venue, technology, or equipment, but a problem with the participants themselves, you will need to take a different approach. If someone isn't having a good time and ap-

▶ Figure 3.5: Use of Unscheduled Room for Unexpectedly Large Group at Library Camp of the West 2008 Breakout Session

proaches you to complain about something that is or isn't happening on the day of the event, there's no need to be defensive. Really listen to the problem, and sympathize as far as seems wise. "I can see how that would be frustrating" might be a useful phrase that allows you to acknowledge your participants' feelings, without necessarily agreeing with their point of view. Ask what they think should be done about the problem. In some cases, they know nothing much can be done, and they are simply looking for the opportunity to register their disapproval. If they are seeking some kind of a solution, see if it is something you think you need to handle or if you are better off asking them to try to implement the solution themselves. This might work especially well when you think that the proposed solution isn't a good one. If the person can convince other people and get a plan together, who are you to say no?

People may also cause problems if they dominate a session by interrupting others or treating it as their own personal bully pulpit. In theory, the session's moderator should be able to restore some kind of balance, but if the domineering person *is* the moderator, that obviously won't work. If you are present for such a session, you might try to simply redirect the focus back to the stated topic: "Hey, that's interesting, but I came to this session because I really wanted to hear about the topic from a variety of viewpoints. Who else has experiences they would like to share?" If that kind of redirection doesn't work, there is always the Law of Two Feet, perhaps this time with a little announcement of where you are headed in case anyone wants to join you. You can't always "save" a session that is going badly, but you can remind people that they are under no obligation to stick around if they feel like their time is being wasted.

▶ BREAK CAMP AND FOLLOW UP

As the end of the day approaches, it is time to think about bringing the unconference to a close in a way that is satisfying for the participants. Even after the day is done, your logistical responsibilities aren't quite over, and you also need to pay attention to the afterlife of the library camp as people think and write and work on what they talked about at the unconference.

Rounding Up

After spending much of the day in breakouts and small discussion groups, the end of the day offers an opportunity for everyone to come back together in a group meeting similar to the one that started the library camp. This ending session can be a kind of "closing ceremonies," which allows a sense of closure and accomplishment for participants. The ending session can also serve as an instant postmortem where the group can immediately evaluate what worked and what didn't work during the unconference while their thoughts and feelings are still fresh. This discussion can, in turn, lead to a discussion about next time. Will you do this again? If so, how should it be different next time?

The closing meeting will have a different energy than the opening meeting did, as people have been talking and working for hours at this point. Some of the participants may have left early to get to other appointments or just to beat the traffic. As with all unconference meetings, remember that those who choose to show up are the right people. These are the people who want to bring the library camp to some kind of closure instead of just dissipating.

For a wide-open, general purpose library camp, there's no need to have a formal "report" for each breakout session. It's difficult to keep people to a time limit, and participants who were really interested in the topic were at the session in the first place. Instead, this is a good time to remind participants that session notes should be posted on the wiki, and that they can check there for any session reports they would like to see. That will also remind people who haven't yet posted their notes to the wiki that they need to do so for the benefit of their fellow participants.

As with any other session at the library camp, you will want to have a record of the suggestions and discussions, so be sure that someone has responsibility for taking notes on this session, too. There's not much point in asking for everyone's suggestions if you aren't going to keep track of them so you can refer back to them some time.

The closing session is a good time for announcements. Some of the announcements might be directly related to what transpired at the unconference, such as new projects or interest groups that participants want to get started based on the day's discussion. But you should encourage people also to announce items that are only tangentially related to the library camp, such as job opportunities, future professional meetings, and upcoming library events.

As the organizer, you may have a few announcements of your own. Remind people of the agreed upon social media tag for the event, so if they plan on writing blog posts or uploading photos or videos they can label all the media with the same tag, allowing it to be easily aggregated and discovered. Remind people who have loaned equipment or supplies for the event to retrieve them. Don't forget to thank your host and any other financial sponsors you might have. Thank your volunteers. Thank everyone who participated (not by name!) because by this point it should be clear to everyone that they created and owned the library camp.

The closing session can also be an occasion to evangelize a bit for unconferences in general. I am usually against evangelism in libraryland, because I think that people who forcefully advocate for a particular idea too often ignore the important differences between individual libraries as they push for their one-size-fits-all solution. In this case, however, the participants have just lived through a unique (or at least unusual) shared experience. You can use this time to point out that now that they know what an unconference is all about, they should be able to pull off their own library camps, too.

If your unconference is a multiple-day event, it may seem like overkill to have a closing session at the end of each day. While you may want to save some things for the last session on the last day, I still believe that a brief ending session on each day of the event will help participants feel more like part of a coherent whole and contribute to a better-integrated experience.

Heading Home

After that, your job is to pack up and go home. Be kind to your host site and pick up any leftover trash, reset tables and chairs as you found them, tear down any signs you posted, and generally use your common sense so that the owners of the site don't end up saying, "this mess was made by a group of *librarians?*"

Pull out the list of borrowed equipment and supplies that you created and make sure you have everything that you are supposed to have. Keep track of what you have actually returned to the rightful owner versus what you have simply collected to take home with you to return to the owner another day. Once you have loaded up any leftover equipment, the day is done! It's time to head out for dinner or drinks or coffee—or home to collapse on the couch.

▶4

MARKETING

▶ **Package the Library Camp**
▶ **Get the Word Out**

Once you have a location, date, wiki, and outline schedule for your library camp, it's time to think about publicity. If you are put off by the idea of "marketing," don't think of it as trying to sell people something. Think of it as letting people know about something wonderful that they might enjoy. The nature of an unconference is such that it will immediately appeal to some people, while others just won't see the point. If you try and spread the word about your event as widely as possible, you will reach more and more of the people in that first category. It's true that "whoever comes is the right people," but marketing will help get you a larger, more diverse group of "right people."

Marketing encompasses the way you package your event—the name, the language you use to describe it, any graphics or other identity you come up with for the unconference—and the way you get that message out to people—word of mouth, online social networking, and so on.

▶ PACKAGE THE LIBRARY CAMP

Before you can start getting your message out there, you need to have a coherent, consistent message to spread. You don't need to think of it as a major advertising campaign, but marketing will be

easier if you approach it with something slightly more sophisti-
cated that "we are having an unconference!"

Name, Description, and Tag

Give your event a unique name. There's no need to get too
cute—some people would argue that "library camp" is a little too
cute to begin with—but decide on a name that is unambiguous
and that you will use consistently when referring to your unconference. A quick look at the LISWiki Library Camp page
(http://liswiki.org/wiki/Library_Camp) shows that most events
have simply been called "Library Camp" or "LibCamp" with the
name of the place and sometimes the date added, as in "Library
Camp Kansas 2009" or "LibCampNYC." If you just call it "Library
Camp," it will be difficult to distinguish from other events when
people are searching the Web for more information about your
particular library camp.

Once you have the name, choose a tag for the event that closely
follows the name. When people are writing about the event online
in blogs, Twitter, or similar media, or posting photos to online
photo sites like Flickr, they can use the tag to help people aggre-
gate all the coverage of the event (see Figure 4.1). A tag should be
short and simple and related to the full name of the event like
"libcampnebraska08" for the 2008 Library Camp held in Nebraska
(see Figure 4.2). With Library Camp of the West 2008, we realized
we had the fortunate accident of the abbreviation "LCOW" so our
tag was "lcow08" and the organizers affectionately called the event
"Ell-Cow."

Remember that your audience may not be familiar with the idea
of a library camp or unconference. Now is the time to look at the
description of the event that you put on the wiki and tighten it up.
Make sure it gets across not just the bland details of the event but
the spirit of the unconference as well. Why is your camp different
from a typical conference? As library camps become more common, you might have to spell out why your camp is different from
other camps, too. If you can boil that down into a paragraph or
two, you will have something that not only works on the un-

▶ Figure 4.1: Flickr Tag

conference wiki but that you can re-purpose when you start getting the word out in other media as well.

For example, in addition to the basic facts about the event (where, when, etc.), we used these paragraphs to help people understand what the Library Camp of the West 2008 was all about:

What Is Library Camp?

Have you ever felt that discussion groups and hallway conversations are the best part of library conferences? Would you rather have a meaningful conversation with a small group of library people than sit and listen to another PowerPoint presentation? Are you interested in sharing ideas about libraries?

Library Camp of the West is an unconference. Instead of creating a schedule of presentations and keynotes in advance, we (that includes **you**) will create a loose plan for the conference on this wiki ahead of time. On the morning of the conference, we'll set the day's schedule and break out into small groups over several sessions based on what attendees want to talk about.

Unconferences work when everyone participates. Come with ideas, notes, examples, visual aids, puppets, whatever. Leave the PowerPoint at home.

▶ Figure 4.2: Library Camp Nebraska 2008 Tags (Photo by Michael Sauers; www.flickr .com/photos/travelinlibrarian/3043083597/)

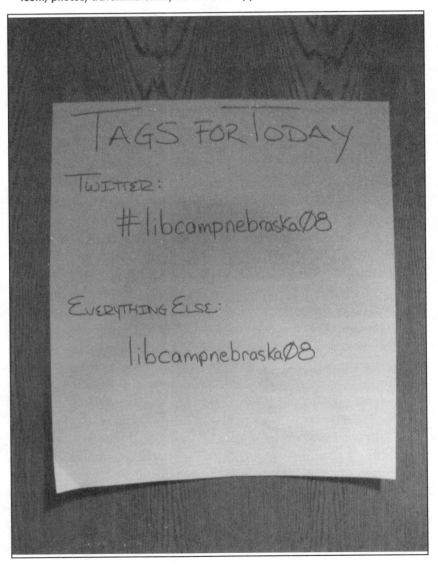

Sounds interesting. What do I do now?

Attendance is free, so put your name on the Attendee Information page (we may have to cap attendance at about 100–150 people). Then suggest a topic to discuss on the Suggested Topics page.

Even that relatively short description may be a little wordy, but it gave us a blueprint to work from when creating e-mail list messages, a Facebook group, and other promotional messages (see "Get the Word Out").

Logo or Graphic Identity

Not all library camps go to the extent of creating a logo or graphic identity for their event. It certainly isn't a necessity; no one will judge the quality of the event based on the logo. But a well-done logo can be a graceful note, a sign that the organizers are thinking of the unconference as a real event. It's also useful to have a graphic that is eye catching and interesting to make your wiki and other online presences look less generic. Repeated exposure to your logo or graphic will help reinforce the event in people's minds.

With Library Camp of the West, we were lucky that I was acquainted with Denver-based comic artist John Porcellino, who agreed to do our "camping cow" illustration for free (see Figure 4.3). But you don't need to hire a professional illustrator for your logo. Just using Photoshop or similar graphics software to set the name of your event in a typeface different from the standard Times or Arial can be a way to create an effective typographic logo (see Figure 4.4).

If you'd rather use a photograph as part of your graphic identity, the photo-sharing Web site Flickr makes it easy for users to assign their photos a Creative Commons license, which allows certain uses of the photo without you even having to ask the photographer first. You can search just the Creative Commons–licensed photographs at www.flickr.com/creativecommons. You will probably want images that don't use the "No Derivatives" license if you

▶ Figure 4.3: Library of the West Logo, by cartoonist John Porcellino

▶ Figure 4.4: Drupal for Libraries Camp (Darien, CT) Logo

plan on cropping, putting type over the image, or making any other changes. If you aren't sure if the license on the image covers the use you have in mind, you can always contact the photographer. The fact that they chose a Creative Commons license to begin with shows that they are interested in people using their photos in some situations. The worst they can do is say "no," and then you can move on and find another picture.

If you do take the time to create a logo, don't be shy about using it. Put it on all your Web pages. Put it on the nametags. Of course, you'll want to put it on any souvenirs or giveaways you decide to hand out. If you print out directional signs for the day of the event, put the logo on those. It will be an immediate visual cue to participants that they are in the right place.

▶ GET THE WORD OUT

It may be just a stereotype, but it seems like librarians are often shy about marketing and publicity. Perhaps it seems too close to sales. I have a friend who says that one of the reasons she became a librarian is so that no one would ever yell at her, "I can't believe you lost the Johnson account!" When publicizing a library camp event, you don't have to worry about that. The library camp will never be everyone's idea of a good time, so there's no point in trying to gain converts. You just need to get the information out there to attract the people who *are* interested. I remember what my father told me about sales: you could try selling a snake door-to-door and 99 people would scream and slam the door in your face. The 100th, though, would call out, "hey honey, the snake man is here!" Selling an unconference is much easier than selling a snake, and you don't need to go door-to-door to do it.

At the other end of the spectrum from the stereotypical shy librarian is the guy who is so excited to share every little project he thinks up that he posts the same hyperbolic message to every e-mail list and social networking site. You know That Guy? Don't be That Guy. Getting your message out doesn't mean you have to turn into a spambot.

To tread the middle path between these two extremes, I suggest that you try to send your message out where you are already a member of the community and that you tailor your message to the particular venue. Start with mailing lists or online communities where you are already a member. People will respond more to a message from someone they already know than they will to a message from someone who just joined up in order to send out a library camp announcement. If there are other groups you want to reach where you aren't a member, try finding an individual in that community who you can get excited about the unconference and get that person to pass the message along. Find out what groups your coworkers are part of, and see if they can send a quick, personalized message to their group.

The more general the group you are addressing, the more generic the message can be. For example, I wouldn't hesitate to join a statewide general library discussion e-mail list and post the description of the event lifted straight from the home page of the wiki. For a more focused group, like an e-mail list for instruction librarians, I might introduce the e-mail by saying, "forgive me if you have seen this announcement elsewhere, but I thought I might suggest a session for this library camp about instruction librarians 'embedded' in semester-long courses. I hope some of you can come." Of course, in order to say something like that, you have to really mean it!

It's safe to say that e-mail lists are still one of the major ways that librarians keep in touch and keep up on professional opportunities, which is why I mention them first. They are likely the way to reach the widest general audience of librarians. But with so many social networking sites and other communications tools on the Web, you should also think about how best to use those sites to promote your library camp. At the moment, Facebook is still popular, especially with academics. It is very easy to set up a Facebook event for your library camp that has all the vital information, your logo, a link to the wiki, and so on. You can also invite people to the event using Facebook, and they can indicate whether they plan to attend or not on the site. If you do that, make sure people know if they have to register elsewhere—you don't want them thinking that accepting the Facebook invitation is equivalent to registering for the unconference.

If you already have a blog of your own, or if you are connected to other librarians on microblogging sites like Twitter or FriendFeed, those are great platforms for mentioning the unconference and pointing people to the Web site. If you aren't connected that way, consider asking someone you know who is connected to post about it. If you want to contact bloggers you don't know personally, I recommend that you make as personal and individual an appeal as you can. You are much more likely to get a positive response if you say something like "I noticed that you have blogged about unconferences in the past. I am organizing this event and wondered if you would want to mention it on your blog (or even attend it in person)" than if you send something that looks like a generic press release. Regardless of how nice and personal you are, many bloggers are very protective of their autonomy, so don't be surprised if they don't take up your cause.

Don't underestimate the value of contacting people personally. When we were in the early planning stages of Library Camp of the West 2008, I made of list of people across Colorado I knew from various committees, mailing lists, and other professional activities. I didn't know all of them very well, but I knew them enough that they'd recognize my name when I e-mailed them. Many of them ended up attending the library camp, and those who didn't were supportive and promised to spread the word at their workplace or to other members of statewide groups.

It's possible that you are thinking, "but I don't know anyone!" First of all, that probably isn't true; ten minutes of brainstorming will probably generate at least a small list of people to notify. But even if it is true, don't worry—after the library camp, you will know a *lot* more librarians.

►5

BEST PRACTICES

- ► **Plan Your Event in Real Time**
- ► **Prepare for Breakout Sessions**
- ► **Follow Up on Your Unconference**

► PLAN YOUR EVENT IN REAL TIME

In Chapter 2, I covered planning for an unconference through use of a wiki and free file-sharing applications such as Google Docs. Other supportive applications used in library camp planning include live planning sessions via online chat and Skype video conference calls.

Chatting Live

E-mail is a great communications tool, but when planning an event as a group, it is a good idea to have a few real-time sessions where you all get together and hash things out. If you are all in the same library or the same town, then it should not be too hard to get everyone in a meeting room (or a restaurant or a bar) for a meeting. If you are spread out, though, you'll want to find a technological solution.

Instant messaging (IM) is a free and easy way to have real-time interaction with your team. Most IM software has some provision for a "group" or "conference" mode. It might be more convenient to use a service that is designed for group chats. Meebo.com is an online service designed to be a multiprotocol instant messenger client, so you can log in simultaneously to, say, your AOL Instant Messenger, Yahoo! Instant Messenger, GTalk, and more, all in the same window. Another popular feature of Meebo is "Meebo Rooms," which allows group chats ranging from two to dozens of users at once (see Figure 5.1). Rooms can be either public and open to all Meebo users or private and limited to users who have the password you assign. You could set up a public room with the name of your event that anyone could enter and participate and view the chat logs of previous chat sessions. If you don't want it wide open, you can also set up a private room that requires a password to participate. Note, though, that private rooms do not preserve chat logs. Instead, you will periodically need to copy and paste the text of your conversation into another document if you want to preserve it.

Another chat-room-style site that is worth investigating is Campfire (http://campfirenow.com), a collaboration tool by the Web design group 37signals. Campfire is similar to IM and Meebo Rooms in that you can type and communicate as a group in real time. With Campfire, you can also upload and share documents

▶ Figure 5.1: Meebo

```
stevelawson@meebo.org: right
stevelawson@meebo.org: so we are going to ask for boardroom stle
newrambler: So how strict do we want to be on the cap for attendance?
stevelawson@meebo.org: er style
stevelawson@meebo.org: and have 35 people around a table
stevelawson@meebo.org: er, 42 people
stevelawson@meebo.org: I assume "boardroom" means "around a central table"
jokrausdu: If the room is set up with tables in a round, then we might not be able to accomodate as many
newrambler: or perhaps 21 people around two tables
jokrausdu: yup.
stevelawson@meebo.org: yeah, I think that's OK
newrambler: I kind of figure people can rearrange furniture somewhat as needed.
stevelawson@meebo.org: if there is anything with overwhelming interest, they can use the ballroom
stevelawson@meebo.org: But I'd be pretty surprised if there was a session that 60 out of 150 people wanted to go to.
jokrausdu: yes, I was thinking the ball room could be a place for breakouts as well.
newrambler: yeah
stevelawson@meebo.org: But I guess that goes to another concern I mentioned of how many things to "track" at the same time.
stevelawson@meebo.org: and, going back to what laura said above
stevelawson@meebo.org: I bet things will get reconfigurd
jokrausdu: what did she say?
jokrausdu: yes.
newrambler: Furniture anarchy.
newrambler: That's what I said.
newrambler: more or less :-)
jokrausdu: I bet we have some technology tracks that might interfere with each other.
jokrausdu: Then again, people will be able to bounce from one room to another.
newrambler: So I'm thinking we announce 1) cap at 150, 2) after that put yourself on the waiting list, 3) if you're not sure and your
arrangements are flexible, please consider putting yourself on the tentative list
stevelawson@meebo.org: right
newrambler: I figure people who live in Denver can perhaps decide to come or not come at the last minute
jokrausdu: Capping at 150 is fine with me.
newrambler: but not so much people from out of state or a ways off in state
jokrausdu: Or way out in WY.
```

and view images right in the flow of the chat. Campfire keeps transcripts of all chats, so you can access them months or years later. Campfire is designed for businesses, and their main model is by paid monthly subscription, with plans from basic to "Max" and prices rising with the number of simultaneous chatters and amount of storage enabled with the account. They do have a free plan, though you might have to hunt around on their pricing page to find it. It allows only four chatters with 10 MB of storage, but that might be sufficient for a small planning committee.

Conference Calling with Skype

Depending on the composition of your group, you might find it easier to dispense with typing little messages and just, you know, *talk* to one another. If there are just two of you, you can use the audio/video chat function of Google's GTalk, but for a group conference call a simple solution is Skype.

Skype is a free application (available from www.skype.com), and calls from one Skype user to another are also free. You can call regular phone numbers, too, but there is a charge for that. At the very least you will need a computer with speakers and a microphone; most people find it works better with a headset that includes earphones and a microphone.

The nice thing about Skype is the immediacy of the conference call. Many people will feel more comfortable communicating by voice than through text. It can be easier than typing in a chat room and provides more direct feedback than a string of e-mails. It is a good way of making sure everyone is on the same page.

The downside is that there will be no written record of your conversation. There is no real need to take notes on IM chats or e-mail exchanges as the conversation is its own transcription. With Skype or traditional phone calls, you will want to take more careful notes. It is possible to record Skype calls with various software plug-ins that are available to purchase.

Keeping Everyone Up-to-Date with E-mail Lists

E-mail has become such a part of our professional and personal lives that it hardly seems like "technology" anymore. But a few best practices for e-mail can make it easier for you to communicate with your planning team and with unconference attendees.

If your planning group is small enough, you might do just fine with direct e-mails sent to the group. Even in a small group, however, this can become problematic when someone forgets to "reply to all" or important messages get deleted. A simple solution is to use an online "group" rather than direct e-mail. Both Yahoo! and Google have a groups section that you can use as an e-mail list and message archive (see Figure 5.2).

Even if the planning group is small enough that you feel you do not need a group mailing list, chances are that the entire group of attendees will be too large to comfortably put on a "bcc:" line in an e-mail. Yes, you will have the conference wiki site and people should be getting most of their information from that, but there will inevitably be announcements, revisions, and reminders (even if it is just a reminder to "check the wiki for details") that will neces-

▶ Figure 5.2: Yahoo Group

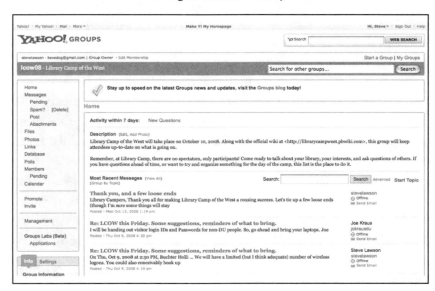

sitate e-mailing your participants. With the Library Camp of the West, we signed people up for the conference mailing list as they registered on the wiki. We let them know that they were being signed up for a list, and in the one or two instances when people really didn't want to be on another list we didn't insist.

Knowing When to Use a Blog

Should you use a blog for your unconference? Isn't the blog the sine qua non of social software and a modern-day Web presence? It seems like it, but the blog falls into an interesting gap when it comes to planning a library camp or unconference.

Unlike a wiki, which is designed for easily editable pages that are organized by topic, the blog's main organizing feature is chronology, with newer entries appearing at the top of the homepage and older entries following until they trail off into the archives. Unlike e-mail, which—for better or for worse—tends to command our immediate attention, it is hard to be sure that your intended audience will revisit the blog or subscribe to feeds of the posts.

That is not to say that blogs have no part in the library camp experience. In Chapter 4, we looked at how you can use existing blogs to spread the word about your event, and later in this chapter we will look at finding blog posts that people write about the experience of attending your library camp. But, when it comes to setting up a new blog that is specifically devoted to your event, I think your effort would be better spent elsewhere.

Using Social Software

What follows is a brief overview of the social software used by Laura Crossett, Joe Kraus, and myself when planning the Library Camp of the West 2008. For a fuller treatment of the topic, see our article, "Collaborative Tools Used to Organize a Library Camp Unconference," in *Collaborative Librarianship* (Crossett, Kraus, and Lawson, 2009).

▶ **E-mail**: For the organizers, our usual e-mail accounts and e-mail clients worked fine (though we sometimes lost the group communication through inadvertently forgetting to "reply to all"). For communicating to people who registered for the camp on the wiki, we used a mailing list on Yahoo! Groups.

▶ **Wiki**: We set up a wiki on PBworks (formerly PBwiki; available at http://librarycampwest.pbwiki.com) three months before the event. We immediately began promoting it and within days had people adding their names to the Registration page and adding ideas to the Suggested Topics page.

▶ **IM**: We would communicate one-on-one via IM as we saw fit, but we also set up a small number of scheduled "meetings" in private Meebo chat rooms. The whole idea was originally hatched in the Library Society of the World Meebo chat room.

▶ **Shared documents**: We used Google Docs to keep track of our to-do list and ideas in one text document and to keep track of our budget and fundraising in a spreadsheet.

▶ PREPARE FOR BREAKOUT SESSIONS

When the library camp is in progress, it is a good idea to be prepared for spontaneous events such as breakout sessions. When a breakout session occurs, success depends on a few key aspects you should provide:

▶ **Moderators**: Either assign them during the creation of the schedule or encourage groups to appoint a moderator as their first point of business.

▶ **Note-taker**: Have at least one, possibly more.

▶ **Visual equipment**: You need to display the notes for all to see on a screen, flip chart, whiteboard, or the like.

▶ **Room configuration**: When practical, set up the room in a circle or a similar configuration that encourages discussion.

▶ FOLLOW UP ON YOUR UNCONFERENCE

Once the event is over, the wiki can still be an active site. People will likely continue to post notes and links to the pages for the individual breakout sessions. You can update the homepage to make it clear that this is a site for an event that already happened. You may want to highlight links to the notes and session reports and downplay the links to things like parking instructions and restaurant maps. I encourage you to leave as much information as possible on the wiki (rather than taking down pages entirely), as your library camp wiki will be a model and an inspiration for future library camp organizers, just as you took inspiration from camp sites that came before you.

Similar to handling the publicity before the event, you will need to handle the posterity of the event. Do your own part to blog about it, post photographs to Flickr or other photo-sharing sites, and e-mail a wrap-up-and-thank-you message to the official unconference mailing list or to other relevant e-mail lists. Encourage other people to do the same, and devote a page on the wiki to linking out to whatever "coverage" of the event you can find. In addition to linking to specific posts or photos that you find, you can also link to searches on Technorati, Twitter, Flickr, and other social software sites to find posts and photographs that use the tag for your library camp.

If you have any left-over bills or other financial arrangements, you need to take care of those as soon as you can after the event. If you have any shortfalls, your sponsors are more likely to respond positively if you ask them right after the event if they can increase their contribution to cover unforeseen costs. It's more likely that library sponsors would respond favorably to such a plea than corporate sponsors, who have already received as much publicity as they can hope to get from the event. If you have a surplus of funds, those can go back to one of your major sponsors with thanks for their being willing to give above and beyond what you really needed.

Regardless of how the finances end up, you should thank your sponsors, co-organizers, and volunteers one more time. A hand-

Finding the Conversation Online

Unconference participants tend to be Internet-savvy and are likely to post blog entries, photographs, and other library camp–related information after (or during) the event. Here are some places to look:

▶ **Flickr**: Try www.flickr.com/photos/tags/[yourtag] to see if people are posting photographs with your conference tag.

▶ **Google Blogsearch**: http://blogsearch.google.com/ will help you find blog posts about your event. Feel free to comment on people's posts, but don't be defensive or angry if you find criticism.

▶ **Twitter**: http://search.twitter.com/ and remember to use the "hashtag" for your conference (usually just the regular tag with a hash mark [#] in front, like #tag).

▶ **Slideshare**: Most of your presenters won't be using slides, but if your event mixes prepared and spontaneous sessions, you might find that some presenters have uploaded their slides to www.slideshare.net. You can "embed" these presentations in another site (like your unconference wiki or a blog post) which can be a good way to provide access to the camp's documentation all in one place online.

written note is nicest and most memorable, but an e-mail is still better than nothing.

Last, in the few days following the event, it's a good idea to collect your thoughts about what went well and what you could improve. You have the comments of the participants from the final session, but you should also be honest with yourself. Putting together an unconference can be a lot of work, and if you were able to provide an occasion for people to meet fellow librarians and have productive discussions about libraries for a day, you should go ahead and pat yourself on the back. Then, on your own and in conversation with your fellow organizers and participants, see what you agree didn't work or could be improved for next time. And don't forget to give yourself time to digest the rest of your conversations from the library camp. You shouldn't have had to spend all your time being the "organizer" of the camp, so let yourself take a few notes and have a few daydreams about your ideas for libraries and librarianship that *aren't* about library camps and unconferences.

►6

MEASURES OF SUCCESS

► **Use the Minimalist Method**
► **Use the Multiple Measures Method**

What makes a library camp a success, and how can you tell if your camp was one? You can tell using one of two methods: the Minimalist Method or the Multiple Measures Method.

► USE THE MINIMALIST METHOD

You will recall that one of the principles of Open Space Technology is "whatever happens is the only thing that could have" (Owen, 2008: 91). Therefore, I offer this minimalist rubric:

Did anything happen at your library camp?
If "yes," your camp was a success.

► USE THE MULTIPLE MEASURES METHOD

Sadly, the Minimalist Method may not satisfy everyone. For an event that has such a wide range of possible positive outcomes, it may be difficult to come up with a single measure of success. Therefore, I suggest that you use some or all of the methods I'll describe. None of them is particularly scientific or quantitative. Instead, they aim to find out what people expected from the event, what they learned, and how satisfied they were.

Using multiple measures will help you get a more rounded view of what happened and how successful it was. Also, don't despair if you don't seem to do well on all of the measures. Some groups will take to some things (like continuing to use the wiki) more than others.

Ask

One of the simplest measures of success is to ask people about their experience while they are still at the event. This is one of the reasons I suggest having a closing session. At that time you can ask people if they think you should do a similar event again, and, if so, what you should change the next time. If you had a very specific theme, it is more likely that people will feel they don't need another event.

Don't worry if people have lots of suggestions for what to do differently next time. If they are interested enough to offer well-thought-out, constructive criticism, it means that they think the library camp is an event worth thinking and arguing about. You may also find that people suggest ideas for changes that you think are terrible ideas or that multiple suggestions contradict each other. That's fine: you are in brainstorming mode at this point, and there is no need to evaluate ideas as they roll in. At the same time, don't make any promises that you will or will not do these things in future events.

Observe

Simply talking to people and listening to participants throughout the day can help you get a sense of what has been working and what hasn't been. In addition, if you are seeing people comparing notes, dividing up sessions, starting discussions in the hallway, and so on, you know things are going as planned. If people seem checked out, disengaged, or are complaining or sitting alone during breaks, perhaps the event did not gel the way that you expected it to.

Compare

There are many reasons why people may need to leave an event early, but the ratio of people who were at the closing session compared to the opening session will give you a rough idea of what proportion of the people attending found the event worthwhile enough to stick around until the end. If people stick around beyond the "end" and chat, exchange contact information, or want to talk to you while you pack up the flip charts, consider that a win.

Monitor the Wiki

The unconference wiki lives on. It doesn't go away at the end of the day. If you are still seeing updates to the site after the event is over, that's a good indication that people wanted to continue the work they started in the session or at least document it all for posterity.

Read the Reviews

If you monitor the tag for your event and keep up with the activity on blogs and other social sites, you will get a good idea of the buzz around the event. If people are mentioning specific conversations they had and sessions they attended and adding their thoughts and ideas online, that's a good indication that the event was stimulating for them. Not all unconferences attract people who are going to blog, tweet, and Flickr their brains out, however.

Consider Your Own Experience

You are the world. You attended this event, right? Out of anyone, you would be the hardest person to surprise. If you still learned things, made new contacts or friends, had a few pleasant surprises, I would consider these good indicators.

If All Else Fails, Break Out the Survey

If you are uncomfortable with the looser measures outlined, it is time for you to write up a survey. You can come up with something fairly simple on paper that you pass out to all the attendees, or you can work something up that is Web based using any number of free online surveying sites. You can ask them to rate different aspects of the day (the location, the food, the number/length of sessions) on a scale of one to five, or very / somewhat / not satisfied. Also save some room for more free-form short-answer questions like these:

▶ What were the best and worst things about the event?

▶ Name a pleasant and an unpleasant surprise.

▶ Would you attend a similar event in the future?

▶ Would you organize a similar event in the future?

▶ If you were going to change three things about the event, what would they be?

Realistically, the best way to understand if your event was a success lies somewhere between the most lassiez-faire "anything is good" attitude and the most buttoned-down "metrics are my co-pilot" philosophy. If the event actually happened, and people actually talked to one another, that's a kind of success. The first time you do anything, it isn't likely to be perfect. Take some time to enjoy that level of success, then go over the multiple measures and see how you will do a better job the next time. Because I predict there will be a next time.

Online Survey Sites

Most of these sites have similar features and offer free accounts with some limitations. When deciding on which site to use, take note of the different levels of service for free and paid accounts. Typically, you may be limited in the number of polls you can run at one time; the number of responses you can collect; how you can download or analyze the results; types of questions and survey logic; and how extensively you can customize the survey's Web page.

▶ Google Docs Forms (http://docs.google.com): If you are already comfortable with Google Docs and especially if you are already using forms for registration or similar tasks, you may find this the easiest way to go.

▶ PollDaddy (www.polldaddy.com)

▶ Survs (www.survs.com)

▶ Twtpoll (www.twtpoll.com): This is for simple one-question polls on Twitter or other social networking sites. It won't allow you to do an in-depth poll, but it's a nice option for something simple.

▶ Wufoo (www.wufoo.com)

▶ Zoomerang (www.zoomerang.com)

REFERENCES AND FURTHER READING

ACRL Unconference 2009. Radical Reference Wiki (March 22, 2009). Available: http://wiki.radicalreference.info/index.php/ACRL_Unconference_2009 (accessed January 19, 2010).

Atkin, Evette. "Library Camp." The unLibrarian Blog (April 15, 2006). Available: http://theunlibrarian.net/blog/?p=6 (accessed January 19, 2010).

Blyberg, John. 2006a. "Camping Out, East Coast Style." blyberg.net (September 28, 2006). Available: www.blyberg.net/2006/09/28/camping-out-east-coast-style (accessed January 19, 2010).

Blyberg, John. 2006b. "Library Camp '06: A Brain-Dump." blyberg.net (April 17, 2006). Available: www.blyberg.net/2006/04/17/library-camp-06-a-brain-dump (accessed January 19, 2010).

Crawford, Walt. "Unconference and Library Camp Practices." Library Leadership Network (July 28th, 2009). Available: http://lln.lyrasis.org/node/353 (accessed January 19, 2010).

> This post by Walt Crawford to the Lyrasis Library Leadership Network site is a very valuable collection of basic information on library camps and unconferences from 2006 to 2008. Using information from library camp wikis and blog posts, Crawford documents the basic information about each unconference, such as when and where it was held, how much advance preparation went into the event, how they

built the agenda, how many people attended, and so on. When possible, he links to blog posts that give more details or personal assessments of how the particular event was handled.

This is only one of several useful articles on unconferences on the Lyrasis Library Leadership Network site. Crawford has also compiled an article on "Unconference Philosophy and Issues" that mixes the voices of librarian bloggers who have written about library camps with Crawford's own observations. The post "Unconferences in Practice: Notes and Resources" excerpts many reports from specific individual library camps.

Crossett, Laura, Joseph R. Kraus, and Steve Lawson. 2009. "Collaborative Tools Used to Organize a Library Camp Unconference." *Collaborative Librarianship* 1, no. 2: 66–99. Available: www .collaborativelibrarianship.org/index.php/jocl/article/view/ 11 (accessed January 19, 2010).

This article by Laura Crossett, Joe Kraus, and myself is a fairly brief rundown of the ways we used online tools to foster our long-distance collaboration when organizing the Library Camp of the West in 2008.

Greenhill, Kathryn, and Constance Wiebrands. 2008. "The Unconference: A New Model for Better Professional Communication." In *LIANZA Conference Papers 2008*. Auckland, New Zealand. Available: www.lianza.org.nz/library/files/store_021/ GreenhillandWiebrands_Unconference.pdf (accessed January 19, 2010).

Greenhill and Wiebrands provide a nice overview of the unconference concept in libraries and also give details from their experiences with several Australian library camps, in particular Library 2.0 on the Loose, held in Perth, Australia, in 2007. They also include the results of a survey of library camp attendees.

LISWiki. "Library Camp." Available: http://liswiki.org/wiki/ Library_Camp (accessed January 19, 2010).

This is likely the most up-to-date listing of library camps and unconferences, at least in North America.

Messina, Chris. 2006. "The Yin-Yang of FOO and Bar." Factory City Blog (August 28, 2006). Available: http://factoryjoe.com/blog/2006/08/28/the-yin-yang-of-foo-and-bar (accessed January 19, 2010).

Momus. "Pecha Kucha: Design Virus." *Wired* (December 19, 2006). Available: www.wired.com/culture/lifestyle/commentary/imomus/2006/12/72321 (accessed January 19, 2010).

Owen, Harrison. 2008. *Open Space Technology: A User's Guide,* 3rd ed. San Francisco: Berrett-Koehler.

Harrison Owen is the original authority on Open Space meetings. Most library camps are using some kind of modified Open Space plan for running their events. Reading Owen's work might inspire you to let go of even more control and make your unconference as open and unplanned as possible. If you are serious about unconferences, this book is required reading.

Rein, Lisa. 2003. "First Movie from Foo Camp: 'Concentrated Foo.'" On Lisa Rein's Radar (October 14, 2003). Available: www.onlisareinsradar.com/archives/001855.php#001855 (accessed January 19, 2010).

Shirky, Clay. 2008. *Here Comes Everybody: The Power of Organizing Without Organizations.* New York: Penguin.

Shirky is a compelling writer and commenter on the Web and online social networking. This book concentrates on how current technologies make it easier than ever to organize groups quickly and without an established hierarchy. Even though he concentrates on the online world, the cultural shifts that Shirky chronicles show that people are more and more open to the idea of spontaneously organized structures and events.

Stephens, Owen. "The Morning after the Mash Before." Overdue Ideas Blog (November 27, 2008). Available: www.meanboyfriend.com/overdue_ideas/2008/11/mash.html (accessed January 19, 2010).

Wikipedia. 2009. "BarCamp." In *Wikipedia, The Free Encyclopedia.* Wikimedia Foundation (May 15, 2009). Available: http://en.wikipedia.org/w/index.php?title=BarCamp&oldid=290022 059 (accessed January 19, 2010).

INDEX

Page numbers followed by the letter "f" indicate figures.

ABOUT THE AUTHOR

Steve Lawson lives in Colorado Springs with his wife, Shanon, and his sons, Luke and Nicholas. Steve is currently the Humanities Liaison Librarian at Colorado College, a small, private liberal arts college where the students take one class at a time for three and a half weeks, then go skiing for a long weekend before starting all over again. It's different.

Steve has a Bachelor of Science in Speech from Northwestern University, where he studied theater, and a Master of Library and Information Science from the University of Texas at Austin's Graduate School of Library and Information Science, where he studied rare books, archives, and special collections. Prior to coming to Colorado College in 2003, Steve worked in the Science and Engineering Library at the University of California, San Diego.

In recent years, Steve's professional interests have included low-overhead, informal methods of professional development for librarians, such as library camps and unconferences and online communities. Steve is co-Carping Nerdboy of the Library Society of the World (LSW), editor of the LSW Zine, sponsor of the LSW Shovers and Makers awards. Steve's next project is likely to look at how the future of librarians was depicted by librarians before the age of the personal computer.